D1545756

Sanctification: Christ in Action

Evangelical Challenge and Lutheran Response

Harold L. Senkbeil

NORTHWESTERN PUBLISHING HOUSE
Milwaukee, Wisconsin

4th printing 1992

Library of Congress Card 88-63671
Northwestern Publishing House
1250 N. 113th St., P.O. Box 26975, Milwaukee, WI 53226-0975
© 1989 by Northwestern Publishing House.
Published 1989
Printed in the United States of America
ISBN 0-8100-0308-2

CONTENTS

For Jane
whose love, constant encouragement,
and occasional prodding
resulted in this book
and continue to demonstrate why she is
the helper fit for me.

Proverbs 31:11

ACKNOWLEDGMENTS

This book could not have appeared without the assistance of many who have helped me identify and formulate the issues challenging the Lutheran Church from the theological right.

Among my teachers I gratefully acknowledge Kurt Marquart, whose course "The Evangelical Sacraments" first launched the pilgrimage I describe in this book; David Scaer, whose New Testament studies have provided fresh insight into the faith "once for all entrusted to the saints," and Robert Kolb, whose sixteenth century "friends" continue to speak eloquently through him to the complex issues of our day.

"The mutual conversation and consolation of brethren," Luther reminds us, is one of the ways God offers his counsel and help (Smalcald Articles IV). Friends I want to thank include Warren Granke, whose theological sensitivity and pastoral heart shed invaluable light on the central issues of this book, and Edward Treptow, whose partnership under the cross has underscored the reality of the new life in Christ.

"Now to him who by the power at work within us is able to do far more abundantly than all that we ask or think, to him be glory in the church and in Christ Jesus to all generations, forever and ever. Amen" (Ephesians 3:20).

All Saints
1 November 1988
Harold L. Senkbeil

INTRODUCTION

This book represents a personal pilgrimage, a pilgrimage into my own spiritual heritage. A Lutheran by birth, by education, and by vocation (now entering my seventeenth year of service as a Lutheran pastor), I have only recently begun to see the great contribution my own church's confession has to offer the Christian mission in our troubled world at the end of the twentieth century.

To many outsiders (for that matter, to many of its own members) the Lutheran church appears to be hopelessly out of step with our world and out of tune with our age. Too liturgical to be easily accessible and too dogmatic to appeal to the diverse religious tastes of our time, Lutheranism is assumed to be incapable of meeting the real needs of our world today without a major overhaul.

Most versions of overhauled Lutheranism look very much like the brand of Christianity that goes today under the heading of "evangelical." Evangelicals have achieved a great deal of success in reaching people in our "me first" age by preaching a subjective gospel, and so Lutherans can hardly be blamed for casting an envious eye in the Evangelical direction.

But, in ridding the Lutheran church of what they see as the excess ballast of its objectivity, its would-be salvagers have very nearly scuttled the ship.

I should know, for I have done my share of ballast-tossing. For the sake of a vibrant gospel, I was willing to ignore and down-play what I now view as the great treasure of my church: its understanding of the means of grace — that is, how God provides people of every age with objective channels by which he comes into real contact with them.

Contact with God is what people in our time desperately seek. Living in an age which has become frightened of and disillusioned with the external world of science and technology, people today are searching inside themselves for answers to the pressing questions of daily life. We all want to know: "How can I know God is real?" "How do I know he is active in my life?" Ultimately, these questions find their focus in one central issue: "Where can I find God?" In other words, *"Where in the world is God?"*

The answer, many evangelical Christians claim, is to be found in the renewed life. In the experience of personal sanctification, the Christian will find convincing proof of God's power and presence. It's no secret that sanctification has not been considered one of the strengths of Lutheran teaching. Evangelical Christianity therefore presents modern Lutherans with a challenge: the challenge to find a meaningful and active relationship with God.

I spoke of a pilgrimage. My pilgrimage began with the conviction that Evangelicals held the only viable key to a committed Christian life. Undertaking a program in graduate theological study, I planned a thesis that would analyze the appeal of Evangelical Christianity and identify the ballast Lutherans needed to throw overboard. Instead, I came to see the great strengths of our incarnational, sacramental heritage in meeting this very challenge. This book is a revision and expansion of that thesis.

I begin with a broad definition and description of the Evangelical phenomenon. The second chapter is a historical sketch of the various theological strains which shape current Evangelical church life in America. Next, I examine three works by a prominent popular New Evangelical author, Charles R. "Chuck" Swindoll. In chapter 3, I summarize Swindoll's own thoughts under various headings. In chapter 4, I analyze Swindoll's teaching on the basis of its own integrity as well as Scripture and the Lutheran Confessions. Finally, chapters 5 and 6 advocate a Lutheran initiative in the face of the Evangelical challenge.

One word to the reader, of whatever theological stripe: This book is not directed *against* "Evangelical Christians." Rather, it is directed *toward* the recovery of a New Testament understanding of the life in Christ which is both thoroughly biblical and absolutely practical. That this description of the Christian sanctified life is also genuinely Lutheran came as somewhat of a surprise to me. It continues to be my personal pilgrimage. And I hope it will be yours.

1

AMERICAN CHRISTIANITY IN THE EIGHTIES: A FOCUS ON LIFE STYLE

The Evangelical odyssey: from backwoods to living room

One of the most astounding developments in twentieth century American Christianity has been the resurgence of the religious right as a force in the theological world. With their Bible-thumping literalism and heartfelt religion, "fundamentalists" seemed to be out of step with a world that had passed them by. They were a source of embarrassment to mainline Christians and an object of ridicule to secular observers. Yet as the century draws to a close, it is the Fundamentalists who appear to be having the last laugh.

Having shed their "country bumpkin" past, Fundamentalists have begun to meet their intellectual opponents on their own ground. They have engaged in a lively debate with both mainline churches and the secular establishment. They have demonstrated that they are a force which must be reckoned with. "Christian" candidates vie for votes in the election process; no campaign manager can ignore the tastes of the conservative Protestant constituency. This is a startling development in the face of what appeared to be the stranglehold liberalism held on political, social and religious views of the nation in the 1960s.

According to American pollster George Gallup, traditional Fundamentalist religious beliefs were widely held in the mid-eighties. Almost half of the people in this nation believe that God created the world within the last ten thousand years, and about one-third believe in the inerrancy of the Bible. Commented Gallup, "The country is much more fundamentalist than I think is generally realized."[1] This kind of evidence demonstrates the vitality of a religious movement long held by the social establishment to be irrelevant, if not extinct.

Obviously, it is difficult to analyze a movement's history while it is still going on. The objective vantage point of the future will provide a more complete picture of the emergence of the "New Evangelicals," as the resurrected Fundamentalists like to call themselves. For now, my goal is simply to describe the Evangelical world in general terms.

In order to understand the term "evangelical," it is helpful to know the background of the word. Lutherans were among the first to wear the adjective "evangelical" — the result of sixteenth century name-calling. Opponents of Lutheran teachers thought they stressed the goods news ("evangel") of Jesus Christ too much, so they called them "evangelical." The name stuck, and it has been worn proudly by succeeding generations. To this day, most Lutheran congregations have an "Ev." somewhere in their official title.

What is usually meant by "evangelical" in modern America, however, describes a theology far different from that of the Lutheran Reformation. Evangelical theology today has many positive features: its focus on the gospel of Jesus Christ, its view of the authority and reliability of the Holy Scriptures and its emphasis on saving souls. However, confessional Lutherans have difficulty with other elements in today's Evangelicalism: its unscriptural emphasis on personal decision in conversion, its spotlight on human experience instead of God's action, and its skepticism about the power of the sacraments.

I mentioned that this book would attempt only a general description of the Evangelical climate. This may be just as well; a picture painted with broad strokes is perhaps the best way to describe a movement which appears to be more form than substance, more style than content, more mind-set than dogma.

Other observers have characterized the world of the New Evangelicals in similar terms. Commenting on the public image of the Evangelical movement, Virginia Owens has remarked:

> . . . they have used the most effective model for communication they know — image advertising. Its success makes old-fashioned apologetics look like an archaeological oddity. Catechisms are replaced by conferences on life style.[2]

A more aggressive critic of "life style Christianity" has produced this stinging evaluation of the proliferation of items such as money guides, sex manuals, quiz shows and other entertainment, all marketed for appeal to the Evangelical consumer:

3

> Christian entrepreneurs began to produce a kind of
> limited mass culture, turning out sanitized copies of
> secular products, a season or two behind the times,
> like discount department store suppliers shaping
> *haute couture* into American sizes. . . . In a sense,
> what these entrepreneurs were creating was not a
> counterculture but a counterfeit culture.[3]

Whether or not one agrees with the judgments
made above, the phenomena they describe are very
much a part of the current religious scene in America. The undeniable fact is that Evangelicalism has a
dramatic impact on the climate of Christianity in
America. To preach and teach the Christian gospel
without taking into consideration this "Evangelical"[4] context of the American religious culture is not
only naive, it is foolhardy. No matter the theological
stripe of their church, people in America's pews in
the latter part of the twentieth century tend to filter
what they hear from the pulpit through Evangelical
lenses.

Lutheran Christians have been feeding on the literature and media of the Evangelicals for some years,
and teaching from Lutheran pulpits is also heard
through Evangelical filters. The language used is
often the same, but the meanings are poles apart.
The late Martin Scharlemann observed:

> Our Lutheran heritage is threatened not only from
> the left, by historical critics and their followers, but
> also from the right, by Fundamentalism [Evangelicalism]. In fact, at the moment, the latter is, by all
> odds, the more menacing because so much of it
> sounds very biblical, and also because so many of our
> fellow conservative Lutherans hear fundamental
> preachers and read "Evangelical" literature with Lu-

theran eyes and ears, so to speak, and thus feel at home in the material.[5]

Fundamentalism has broken free of its backwoods exile; it is now a very respectable guest in America's living rooms. The theological shoe, so to speak, is on the other foot. Now it is the liberal mainline church establishment that seems antiquated. Richard John Neuhaus comments on how things have changed since the Scopes "monkey trial" of the twenties:

> ... it is the certitudes of Clarence Darrow which now seem pitiably quaint, while the future is claimed by high-tech religious communicators who style themselves the American Coalition for Traditional Values. Little wonder that sectors of our cultural leadership show every sign of having gone into cultural shock.[6]

The question is, how can we account for the Evangelical odyssey? What is to explain the tremendous upsurge in popularity of a theology that only a few years ago was belittled as hopelessly backward and narrow? Part of the explanation is undoubtedly the complex environment in which Americans find themselves.

The climate of our age: anxiety/isolation

Undeniably, one of the great issues faced by civilization in our time is the threat of global doom. The specter of nuclear warfare, environmental pollution, the AIDS epidemic, and other impending disasters have all given Americans the distinct impression that they are living on top of a powder keg of destruction. The certainties proclaimed from Evangelical pulpits have an understandable attraction for people living in the midst of such uncertainties.

When coupled with the millennial view prominent in many Evangelical circles, these certainties provide a way to make sense out of a world seemingly gone out of control. Taking its cue from the thousand year reign of Christ described in Revelation chapter twenty, millennial thought teaches that Jesus will one day return to set up a kingdom of peace, prosperity and security for believers here on earth. This aspect of the Evangelical attraction has not gone without notice even outside of its own circles. A prominent Jewish author writes, "The new chiliastic (millennial) religions and cults provide a wide variety of answers in a world of doubt, certainty in a world of uncertainty, and belief in a world of competing facts."[7]

If there are global issues to raise their fears, today's Americans are also contending with some very real personal issues. The divorce rate is at an all-time high. The fundamental roots of society have come under attack, thus injecting personal instability into lives already reeling under the external stresses mentioned above.

Added to this basic instability in the fabric of individual lives is the stress of our fast-paced life style and highly mobile society. Peoples' jobs are taking them away from those extended family members who used to provide identity and context in their lives as well as support in times of distress. Just when there is a greater need for security and support from other people, today's Americans are finding themselves more and more alone.

The very technological developments which promised a better quality of life have actually increased the isolation in which Americans live their lives. Personal computers and high tech entertainment such as VCRs tend to isolate people in their own electronic worlds. Increasingly we see people wearing portable radio/tape players oblivious to the public around them, immersed in the sounds they hear in their private earphones.

Jeremy Rifkin has underlined the ironic predicament of the consumer society:

> We live an anonymous existence, our only common bond being the vast consumer fantasyland of indulgences from which we pick and choose our playthings. Our lives now revolve around the shopping center — the place where more people spend their leisure hours than anywhere else.[8]

This famine of human interaction has created a hunger for the personal touch, and indications are that the American public is sensing its hunger pains. Recent years have seen a rising market for self-help books with a distinctive new thrust. No longer focusing only on personal development, more and more books now stress interaction with others. The subject of friendship is but one example. Although a few years ago few books were being written on this topic, at this writing such books appear to be in an upsurge of popularity.

To people increasingly aware of their loneliness, Evangelical Christianity offers the warmth and love of the caring Christian community. Here, in the fellowship of the Body of Christ, the lonely find not mere companionship, but genuine oneness. Here people are made to feel important; here they are not simply tolerated, but prized.

The importance of Christian fellowship can hardly be discounted as a key factor in the popularity of Evangelical churches today. Parish pastors of all denominations have become increasingly aware of the "friendliness factor" as people look for churches in their new community. Most observers of American church life see this factor as more important than denominational loyalties for people who are choosing new church homes.

The Evangelical attraction: personal experience as proof of faith

It is not difficult to see the attraction of Evangelical theology for people today who are struggling with anxiety and isolation. In the Evangelical family, many have found instant community, personal worth and acceptance.

A comprehensive critique of current Evangelical theology is outside the narrow focus of this book. But some minimal observations might be made. Three factors appear to be at the heart of the tremendous upsurge in popularity of the Evangelical movement in American church life today:

1. The uncertainty of our time.

In a world with so much uncertainty, it is not surprising that people would be turning to a brand of Christianity that answers their questions and takes its stand not on the shifting sands of human speculation, but on the solid rock of divine revelation.

2. The anxiety of our world.

In a world with so much anxiety, it is not surprising that people find a great attraction in Evangelicalism, with its emphasis on eternal salvation in heaven. Since we are not sure how long this world can continue, it is comforting to know that though this world is passing away, the heavenly mansions are waiting.

3. The loneliness of our lives.

In a world where people exist in insulated isolation, it is not surprising they would find the caring concern emphasized by the Evangelical church extremely attractive. People are longing for the human touch in a dehumanized world, and increasingly they seem to be finding it in Evangelical churches.

These pragmatic concerns, no doubt, explain much of the rise of Evangelicalism. In large part, these concerns must be dealt with in a realistic way by any church wishing to be faithful to the Lord and his gospel in our age.

One additional factor in the rise of Evangelicalism, however, raises serious concerns for anyone concerned about faithfulness to the biblical gospel:

4. The triumph of subjectivism.

In our relativistic age, the validity of any concept is not in its truth by some objective standard, but in its meaning for the individual. A wide variety of goods, ranging from hamburgers to automobiles, are advertised with an appeal to personal self-interest. The consumer is reminded that what is best for him is best: "You deserve a break today" and "Have it your way."

Our society appears to be more concerned with subjective meaning than objective truth, even when it comes to moral values. Instead of searching for objective standards upon which to base action in today's complicated moral issues, American society is much more interested in achieving a consensus of opinion. "I feel" has been substituted for "I think." The obvious subjective thrust of Evangelical theology is tremendously attractive to such a world view. The individual who has "invited Jesus to come into his heart" has no need to substantiate the truth of his convictions. He "feels" like a Christian, and for him that is the most important part of believing. The ultimate absurdity of this approach to the Christian faith is best expressed in the words of the old gospel hymn:

> You ask me how I know he lives?
> He lives within my heart!

Richard Quebedeaux's evaluation of the practical function of "spiritual gifts" as evidence for the truth of the Christian faith holds true for the general Evangelical experience as well:

> In a word, charismatic renewal has been a celebration in our generation that God has not forgotten his promises, that he is, in fact and deed, a living God, totally committed to work in evidential ways through the lives of those committed to him.[9]

Whether the focus is on speaking in tongues or conquering a pet sin, Evangelical Christianity regards these human actions as a demonstration of God's reality in the human experience. In our subjective age, the attraction of this brand of demonstrable Christianity can hardly be underestimated.

The Lutheran focus: the word of the gospel

Lutherans find themselves on foreign territory when subjective feelings or human activities are held to be the basis of faith. Scripture and the Lutheran Confessions are full of references to the subjective results of the gospel in the life of the believer, but never are these regarded as the source of certainty for our salvation. This New Testament insight is not a theological abstraction; it was handed on to us because of the intensely personal struggle of a sixteenth century German monk, Martin Luther.

Luther's quest for peace with God led him to see the bankruptcy of every attempt to find assurance in the heart or life of man. He came to see that there could be only one source of certainty: the objective word of the gospel. In his valuable study of the theology of Luther, Walther von Loewenich writes:

> Peace is not to be sought by way of empirical experience, as pietism thinks. According to Luther, that would be tempting God. For in that way we would forsake the stance of faith and attempt to have peace in physical reality rather than in faith. But we also have Christ, who is our peace, only by faith.[10]

The Lutheran Confessions are unequivocal in their rejection of God's operation in the heart of man apart from the objective means of grace:

> Condemned are the Anabaptists and others who teach that the Holy Spirit comes to us through our own preparations, thoughts and works without the external word of the gospel. (Augsburg Confession, V, 4)[11]

It is important to note that this message is objective ("external"), real ("word") and powerful ("of the gospel", i.e., offering forgiveness). For certainty of faith, the believer must look outside himself to that

11

word of the gospel: "the promise of forgiveness of sins and justification because of Christ." (Apology IV, 43)

A major section of this study will be devoted to the exposition of a Lutheran approach to sanctification.[12] For now, it may be noted that the link between God and the believer is never the believer's own feelings, but the Person of Jesus Christ, God's Son, who comes to us in his gospel. Jesus is himself the word of the Father made flesh.[13] In the word of his gospel, he has promised his continuing presence and power with his church.[14] To search for confidence of a right relationship with God in one's own life or in the feelings of the heart is to introduce a concept alien to the gospel and detrimental to the faith. Luther had an apt term for the horrible danger which comes from basing our faith on anything inside of us: *monstrum incertitudinis*, "the monster of uncertainty."[15] It is a monster which continues to threaten Christians in every age, a monster which can be conquered only by the external promises of God in Jesus Christ!

The Evangelical focus: a question of life style

Evangelicalism is very difficult to confine within one unified theological system; a wide range of beliefs comes under its umbrella. From the old-fashioned, southern style Bible thumping of Jerry Falwell through the sophisicated erudition of Robert Schuler's religious pop psychology, American Evangelicalism presents a bewildering array of doctrinal emphases.

A more useful unifying principle lies not in the doctrine of Evangelicalism, but in its practice: to be an Evangelical in America today is largely a question of mindset and style of personal piety. Evangelical identity is established more on the basis of which books are read, which religious terms are laced into conversation, and what language is used in public prayer than on what specific doctrines are believed. Nearly twenty years ago, long before Evangelicalism had climbed from notoriety to acceptance, Bruce Shelley observed: "Evangelical Christianity is not a religious organization. It is not primarily a theological system. It is more of a mood, a perspective and an experience."[16]

The focus of the Evangelical spotlight on life style leads to the central thrust of this book: that Evangelicals present their greatest challenge to Lutheran theology in the area of sanctification. I cannot emphasize enough that this is far more than a doctrinal issue; this is also a cultural issue. We have to recognize that we live in an Evangelical world; for the past ten to fifteen years Evangelical values, habits and tastes have taken over the public spotlight.

The popular piety of Evangelicalism has assumed the central role as a pattern for the practice of the Christian life in America. Evangelicals have succeeded in breaking down the gates of the "secular city," as western civilization was characterized only two decades ago. Some have deliberately set about completing John Calvin's dream of building a society governed only by Christian principles. Others simply wish to "let their lights shine." The results have been simply astounding:

> In Orange county, one of the chosen places of evangelicalism, it was possible to dwell in a total Chris-

tian environment. Letting their fingers do the walking through the *Christian Yellow Pages*, evangelicals could buy a car from a born-again dealer, get their taxes prepared by a devout CPA, get their necks uncricked by Christian chiropractors, consult Christian lawyers for Christian divorces, purchase their fashions from a Revelation outlet, get their carpets cleaned by a Christian-operated hydro steam unit, have their coiffures trimmed at Hair After, have their pools cleaned by New Life Pool Maintenance, have their drains unclogged by Agape Plumbing, and get their pests fumigated by Golden Exterminators, Inc.[17]

It could be asked, of course, what makes a plumber a "Christian plumber"? Most inhabitants of the popular Evangelical world would not mean by the term a plumber who happens to be a Christian, but rather a *born-again*[18] Christian who happens to be a plumber. Professional credentials are evaluated on the basis of conformity to the forms of practical piety expected in Evangelical circles, not on the basis of skills in the profession.

It is easy to see that what has developed under the guise of the practice of the Christian faith borders on a new monasticism. People circulate in their own tightly knit circles of like-minded Christians, surrounding themselves all the while with the trappings of the "Christian" life style.

This monastic approach to the faith has not met with universal approval. Though it is held up by some to be the ultimate in Christian spirituality, in reality it is a form of cultural isolationism. Evangelical authors themselves have asked whether instead of making the secular sacred, the New Evangelical life style has actually secularized the sacred:

The proliferation of religious books, however, has come about not because more and better books are being written but because there is a statistically predictable market for them. Cookbooks, diet books, exercise books, sex books, money books, sports books, psychology books. Every element that can be abstracted from secular culture to bolster the Christian culture. We are awash in a sea of supposedly Christian information. Thus have we succeeded in trivializing the infinite.[19]

The Evangelical challenge: sanctification that works

In our pragmatic age, people are much more prone to ask "does it work?" than "is it true?" The assumption is made that if it works, it must be true. More fascinated with results than theory, contemporary Americans are understandably impressed with Evangelicalism. Here is a theory which seems to work; here is a theology which appears to bring results. God is at work in the world: the believer has only to look to his own life to see the reality of his commitment to Christ working its way out in demonstrable ways. This is no "paper god"; this is the living Lord of heaven and earth! In the lives of his people, it is held, God demonstrates his power in living reality:

> With some people, we can actually feel a spiritual presence, a sort of glow which remains even after the person has left. They speak as if someone else were speaking through them. This is the glory, the transformation, the transfiguration, the new life — the supernatural life which God gives to us.[20]

It will not do simply to criticize the blatant sensuality of such remarks, as if Christianity were a matter of the head only, and not the heart as well. To the Evangelical mind one thing matters: here we have a handle on practical Christianity, the "how-tos" of the faith. No more speculation or theory; here in the heart and life of the believer we find God! Everyone is looking for God, and so we also find Lutheran minds and hearts succumbing to a theology which is at its core Reformed and Fundamentalist. The attraction is irresistible: here, in Evangelical teaching and practice, is a sanctification that seems to work. This is far more than just memorizing the teaching of Luther's *Small Catechism* that the Holy Spirit "calls, gathers, enlightens, and sanctifies... " nor even that Jesus Christ "is my Lord ... that I may be his own, and live under him in his kingdom, and serve him. . . . " Instead of empty memorization, Evangelicals offer action. Here you can find fervor, not only intellectual affirmation. Here one can see action, and not just talk. Here there are disciples, not merely members! This is the Evangelical challenge to Lutheran theology: a sanctification which really works! In the words of one former Lutheran:

> Here (in the Assembly of God Church) I have found people who really care about me. Here I have met people who will pray with me. Here I have seen God at work in my life, helping me to overcome my quick temper. Here I can sense God's presence.[21]

This is not the first time in history Reformed theology has presented a challenge to Lutherans on this issue. Many pioneer German Lutheran settlers fell prey to the attraction of the "practical" Christianity they observed among German-speaking churches of the revivalist/pietistic strain. The father of the Lutheran Church—Missouri Synod, Dr. C. F. W. Walther, recognized the challenge for what it was:

> When our naive brethren arrive in America and observe the saintly exterior of the sectarians, how sincerely they pray, weep and sigh, they conclude this must be the true church. In Germany they had frequently seen clergymen who were belly-servers, whose chief concern was their income.... They spoke only of the price of grain, hogs, and the like. It is not surprising, then, that these poor people, observing the saintly appearance of an enthusiast, would conclude: "This is a totally different sort of person. He wants to save people. Here is the true church."[22]

Walther's response was not merely defensive. His concern was not to protect Lutheran quietism in the face of pietistic activism and fervor. Rather, he seized the initiative in demonstrating the shallowness of revivalist preaching and at the same time the inherent connection between the doctrine of the Lutheran church and a living, vital Christian faith. Over a period of thirteen years (1873-1886) he delivered a lengthy series of essays under the theme: "The Doctrine of the Lutheran Church Alone Gives All Glory to God, An Irrefutable Proof That Its Doctrine Alone Is True." Meeting the sectarian challenge on its own ground, he contended that the acid test for any theology is its end result: does it seek man's glory or God's glory? Proceeding to deal with twelve different biblical doctrines,[23] Walther demonstrated that Lutherans need not take a back seat to anyone when it came to glorifying God in every teaching.

I contend we need a similar Lutheran response to the contemporary challenge. Please remember: this is not a game of theological "one-upmanship." I am not interested in "Evangelical bashing." Rather than responding in a defensive way, we need a new Lu-

17

theran initiative in demonstrating the dynamic truth *and practicality* of our scriptural doctrine for every Christian's life. It's high time we dusted off the tools of our rich spiritual heritage and put them to work in peoples' lives.

The big question today is: "Where in the world is God?" The standard Evangelical answer falls short. The reality of God is to be found not in its dim reflection on the shifting sands of the human heart, but in the objective truth of the gospel, anchored in the Word made flesh and made available to people of every era through the means of grace. What could be more "Evangelical" than that?

2

THE ROOTS OF
EVANGELICALISM

The story of the American religious journey is both
fascinating and perplexing. The sheer number of theological strands woven into the tapestry of American
Christianity is impressive, even though its complex
pattern is bewildering at times. In this chapter I attempt to trace some themes and movements which
have preceded American Evangelicalism. If some
readers find this a frustrating experience, please remember that unraveling a tapestry can be not only
frustrating but also destructive. Once we have separated it into its parts, it no longer exists; that's where the
frustration comes in! Just as tapestries are more than a
conglomeration of threads, so also Evangelicalism is
more than the sum of its parts. I realize I am taking
apart what is now a cohesive whole, but dissection is
the only way to find out how an organism functions.

To use another analogy, the various streams of theological influence have blended with each other as they
converged into the river of Evangelicalism. The Ameri-

can church is on a journey down that river, but I'm inviting you to travel in the other direction — to join me on an expedition into its headwaters. I hope you will find it as much of a discovery as I have!

The New England Calvinists

The first stream in the river of American Evangelicalism we explore is New England Calvinism. Here in the rich soil of the colonial work ethic and the fierce spirit of independence, Calvinism grew and flourished. The fruit it bore included a whole system of American higher education (e.g., Harvard and Yale Universities) and an indelible stamp upon generations of Americans to come, no matter what their theological stripe. Here were the foundations for the kind of rugged individualism and sense of destiny that have come to characterize the "American dream." It is not possible to this day to practice the faith in this country without being confronted with the peculiarities of American Christianity, largely a product of its Calvinist forebears over two hundred years ago. The great patriot and redoubtable deist, Benjamin Franklin, was merely reflecting the influence of Calvinism when he coined the proverb which has nearly become the sacred motto of Americans: "God helps those who help themselves."

Certainly the founding fathers of American religion held to traditional Calvinist teachings, including double predestination (God predestined some to heaven and others to hell) and limited atonement (Christ did not die for everyone). These doctrines are today almost totally extinct, victims of the kind of vigorous Arminianism[1] that has come to describe the position of most of American Protestantism.

Though damaged by the disillusionment of the 1960's, the sense of divine destiny for America which figured prominently in early American Calvinist though still lingers on. It can certainly be detected most clearly in the vocal demand of the religious right.[2] The religious right is noted particularly for its political activism, as well as its theological conservatism. Even in the less strident voices of the more sophisticated Evangelical media, one can still detect echoes of the voice of the eminent governor of Massachusetts Bay Colony, John Winthrop. Before setting foot on the shores of the new land, he exhorted his fellow colonists aboard the *Arbella*.

> Wee are entered into covenant with [God] for this worke. . . .Now if the Lord shall please to heare us, and bring us in peace to the place wee desire, then hathe he ratified this covenant . . . but if wee shall neglect the observation of these articles . . . and . . . shall fall to embrace this present world and prosecute our carnal intentions seeking great things for ourselves and our posterity, the Lord will surely break out in wrath against us, be revenged of such a perjured people and make us knowe the price of the breach of such a covenant.[3]

The words of this sermon could well serve as an introduction for the discussion of all of American history, since the American experience can hardly be understood apart from Calvinist covenant theology. Simply put, its thesis is this: If we keep our end of the bargain, God will keep his. If we act as his people, he will act as our God. If we fulfill his will, he will bless us. If we violate his will, he will punish us. It must be stressed that this is understood not only as an individual covenant, but as a collective covenant: this is God's agreement with America!

That this covenant idea has endured through the dark days of Viet Nam and Watergate is a testimony to its tenacity. Governor Winthrop's prophetic words still ring in the regular and insistent calls for national repentance issued by leaders of the present religious right.

Still more tenacious than this idea is its corollary: If God is pleased with us, we can see it in his blessings in our lives. Though they were thorough-going Calvinists on the sovereignty of God and the inscrutability of his divine (and double)[4] predestination, the Puritan fathers believed in "experienced predestination." They held that the divine favor of election was demonstrated in the believer's religious experiences.

Here was the fertile theological soil which, nourished by other developments discussed below, led to the great emphasis among today's American Evangelicals on sanctification as demonstrated in the Christian's inner life.

The Arminian revivalists

By the end of the revolutionary war, Calvinism was firmly entrenched as the dominant force in American church life. The Congregationalists, Presbyterians and Baptists, together with a sizeable number of the Episcopalians, were the theological heirs of the Puritan colonial fathers. On the issues of election, conversion and covenant, American Protestantism was monolithic in its Calvinist viewpoint.[5] Together, these denominations comprised some twenty-two hundred congregations scattered along the Eastern seaboard.

All was not well in the American Zion, however. Despite the current myth of "Christian America," the fact is that by the close of the Revolutionary War American church life was at a low ebb. Such prominent citizens as Benjamin Franklin and Chief Justice Marshall expected that organized Christianity would soon go out of existence. Some estimate that church membership in the 1780s was about ten per cent of the population.[6]

In the last decade of the eighteenth century winds of revival began to blow across the land. The decline of American Christianity reversed as thousands were added to the churches of Virginia, New England and the Kentucky frontier.[7] Fueled by the kind of religious subjectivism that characterized the cross-cultural revival in the early 1700s both in Europe and America, this "Second Great Awakening," as it was called, brought with it a shift in the focus of preaching. No longer were pulpits dedicated to John Calvin's covenant theology emphasizing what God had done; now the emphasis was clearly on man's end of the bargain.[8]

No longer could the Christian regard himself as a simple recipient of the irresistible grace of God, unconditionally elected by God's sovereign will, as the Calvinists had decreed in the Canons of Dort (1619). This classic statement of the Calvinist position had been drawn up in Holland to counter the Remonstrance Movement and its chief spokesman, Jacobus Arminius. It was in America, a century and a half later, that Arminius was to have his final triumph. His was a theology which fit the American frontier. Here people were the actors, not mere recipients.

Here a people could take their personal welfare into their own hands. After the revivals of the late 1700s and the early 1800s, the free will of man in conversion was an incontrovertible truth for most American Protestant Christians.

> After (Jonathan) Edward's time revivalist theology in America moved steadily toward emphasizing the human side of religious experience. This tendency was manifested in various ways of positing the free and decisive character of the human free will. Free will was virtually an American dogma; indeed it was practically an unassailable article of faith for most of western culture. It was also a concept that was a great aid to evangelism, which seemed most effective when based clearly on personal "decision."[9]

The most prominent force in the religious revival of the 1800s was Charles Finney. After his conversion in 1821, he was sent by the Presbyterian church as a missionary to the frontier. There he began to introduce what his shocked Calvinist superiors called "new measures" in his preaching. A successful trial lawyer before his conversion, he began to emphasize techniques designed to elicit dramatic responses from his hearers. These included shouting at individuals in the congregation by name and inviting convicted sinners forward to the "anxious bench," to await the moment of grace when, after much vocal turmoil, they would achieve personal salvation by the decision of faith.[10]

Though such methods were effective on the raw frontier, they were despised by the Presbyterian leadership on both theological and aesthetic grounds. The great Calvinist cleric, Lyman Beecher, had threatened his active opposition all the way through

New England, but ended up inviting Finney to his own sophisticated pulpit in Boston. In time, Finney won wide-ranging support from the urban intellectual and financial power centers for his backwoods mission. More significantly, Finney's triumph signaled the final defeat of classic Calvinist doctrine in the area of conversion. Now it was held that anyone could be saved; furthermore each person had the responsibility to decide for himself to accept Christ or to be damned forever. It is possible to trace American revivalism all the way from Finney (d. 1875) through Dwight L. Moody (d. 1899) and Billy Sunday (d. 1935) to Billy Graham as an unbroken chain of emphasis on personal decision in salvation.

Whereas the earlier Awakening of the opening decades of the eighteenth century took place largely in a Calvinist framework, the second Great Awakening was primarily Arminian in scope and format. The shift in focus is easily detectable, for example, in the hymns of revivalism. Rather than the awful majesty of God and the magnitude of his grace featured in the hymns of the early eighteenth century, the "gospel hymns," as they were called, focused on the emotions of those who meet Christ by the personal decision of faith. This heritage of the popular piety of revivalism is still evident in modern Evangelicalism. The spotlight is still very much on the subjective feelings of the believer, rather than on the majesty and grace God.

The infusion of Arminianism served to revitalize an American Protestantism that had grown feeble. Its activist stance appealed to the spirit of the age: expansionist, individualistic, aggressive. Less than a hundred years after Justice Marshall predicted the total collapse of the American church, a prominent Evangelical could boast of Christianity's triumph over rationalism:

> At no time has Christianity been assaulted with such variety and persistency of argument as during the hundred years just passed. . . . Never since the crucifixion has the religion of Christ, in its purest forms had a stronger hold on the popular heart than at this day.[11]

The march of revivalism in the United States was vigorous and it was complete. So strong was the hold of revivalist theology in American Christendom that one observer is able to state unequivocally: "In the nineteenth century, revivalism was not a type of Christianity in America; it was Christianity in America."[12]

Besides the emphasis on personal decision, revivalism has bequeathed to its modern Evangelical heirs a tendency to regard earthly success as a mark of divine approval. The great revivalist preacher Dwight L. Moody once asserted:

> It is a wonderful fact that men and women saved by the blood of Jesus rarely remain subjects of charity, but rise at once to comfort and respectability. . . . I never saw the man who puts Christ first in his life that wasn't successful.[13]

Here we have the seeds of the kind of theology of success propounded by many in today's electronic church.

It is not difficult to see the parallels between Arminian revivalism and modern Evangelicals in both theology and methodology. Not only the emphasis of today's Evangelicals on personal decision, but the style and ethos of their ministry reflect the early American evangelistic pioneers of the second Great Awakening. If it is true that being an Evangelical in America today is more a state of mind than a doctrinal position, we can see the beginnings of that mindset in the revivals of the eighteenth and nineteenth centuries.

The European Pietists

The influence behind the religious revivals of the eighteenth and nineteenth centuries in America is found in another century and on another shore. The very terminology *second* Great Awakening which is applied to the series of revivals we have discussed implies a prior movement, which is more properly called *the* Great Awakening. Though its effects were noticed in the new land, its source was in the old homelands of England, the Netherlands, and primarily in Germany. Here, among the theological descendants of Martin Luther, a reawakening of spirituality arose that has come to be known as Pietism.

Pietism arose within the context of a German Lutheran orthodoxy which appeared to have grown too cold and formal to have any effect on the Christian's life. Pietism's focus from the beginning was on the inner life and the subjective experiences of the heart as an aid toward a living, vibrant commitment to Christ that showed itself in action. Its founder, Philipp Jakob Spener (d. 1705), was a pastor in Frankfurt who was deeply concerned about the spiritual laxity he saw among Lutheran clergy and laity. Borrowing ideas he had observed in Reformed circles during his student days, he instituted a rigorous discipline in the life of his congregation built around personal Bible study, prayer and mutual exhortation through small groups which met in his home, which he called *collegia pietatis* ("assemblies of the faithful"). The purpose of these groups, Spener wrote, was:

> ... to establish among Christian individuals a holy and close friendship, that each one learns to recognize the Christianity of the others whereby the fire of love is more and more inflamed among us, from which so much passionate desire arises that everyone may be edified at every opportunity and by their example may excite others next to them to heartfelt earnestness.[14]

Here in Spener's own words it is possible to see the destination of the theology of Pietism, if not its point of departure. The language used is a good indication of its direction: "the fire of love . . . inflamed," "passionate desire . . . arises," "excite . . . to heartfelt earnestness." Here the message is evident in its media. The main goal of these *ecclesiolae in ecclesia* ("little churches within the church") is clearly different from that of the Reformation. The focus here is not the external word of the gospel, but the internal workings of the sanctified heart.

Spener's efforts at ridding the church of what he saw as a dead orthodoxy were resisted by church authorities, but received with widespread popularity among the laity. Finally, upon an appointment to a Berlin pulpit, he found a stable platform from which to spread the Pietistic reform.

As often happens in ideological and theological movements, Spener's followers went beyond his teachings. Spener had held the teachings of his Lutheran church in high regard and retained a formal allegiance to Lutheran orthodoxy. Many of those who came after him had little use for what they saw as cold abstractions. The interest of Pietism was increasingly on the inner strivings of the heart and the subjective experience that it called "new birth." Mingling their concerns for the sanctified life with certain strains of medieval mysticism, some Pietist leaders fostered a highly developed devotional life. Prominent among them was Count Nicolaus von Zinzendorf (d. 1760). At Herrnhut, his religious colony in Moravia, he developed a tightly woven society with a piety centering on the contemplation of Jesus' suffering. In contrast to Luther's theology of the cross,[15] however, here the passion of Christ was interpreted in a highly emotional and exclusively subjective way. The desire was that by meditation on the suffering of Jesus, particularly his blood and his wounds, the devout would so identify with Jesus' feelings that they themselves would achieve the inner feeling of release from sin.

John Wesley (d. 1791), an Anglican priest, is the link between European Pietism and American Revivalism. His search for the deeper spiritual life began while he was a student at Oxford. At a meeting of like-minded friends in a house on Aldersgate Street in London on the evening of May 24, 1738, he was listening to the reading of Luther's Preface to the Book of Romans and experienced what he regarded to be his personal renewal:

> I felt my heart strangely warmed. I felt I did trust in Christ, Christ alone for salvation; and an assurance was given me that he had taken away my sins, even mine.[16]

Following his conversion, Wesley began a campaign for spiritual renewal, first within the Church of England, and then after his rejection, outside it. Since his spiritual interest had been first heightened by his interaction with Moravian missionaries while on a trip to colonial America, he journeyed to Herrnhut to learn strategies for renewal from von Zinzendorf.

Thus Wesley became the link between the German Pietism represented by the great founder of the Moravians and the revivalism in America, for in 1784 Wesley appointed Thomas Coke and Francis Asbury as "superintendents" to a mission in America. Here the sensationalist tactics of the Wesleyan preachers met with great response, and within a decade Methodists, as their adherents were called,[17] had built one of the largest church bodies in America.

Pietism had flung down the gauntlet. The state churches in Europe and the established Calvinist denominations of America had been issued a clear challenge on the issue of certainty of salvation.[18] A person might say that he or she was a Christian, but that didn't prove anything. Outward conviction was not enough. The road to certainty was to be found in the experienced emotions of the sanctified heart. "Yes," the Pietists were saying, "you may think that you believe, but that is not enough. What you need is a new heart; Christ must dwell in your hearts by faith."

This was not the first time such a challenge had been issued. Already in Luther's time some of his radical students felt he had not gone far enough in ridding himself of the baggage of Rome. The assurances of the external Word were not enough, they contended. What was needed was the cultivation of the new life and the inner light of the Spirit, which they believed was given apart from the Word and sacraments. Luther's response was carefully reasoned and scripturally balanced:

> Now when God sends forth his holy gospel he deals with us in a twofold manner, first outwardly, then inwardly. Outwardly he deals with us through the oral word of the gospel and through material signs, that is, baptism and the sacrament of the altar. Inwardly he deals with us through the Holy Spirit, faith and other gifts. But whatever their measure or order the outward factors should and must precede. The inward experience follows and is effected by the outward. God has determined to give the inward to no one except through the outward. For he wants to give no one the spirit or faith outside the outward Word and sign instituted by him, as he says in Luke 16, "Let them hear Moses and the prophets." Accordingly Paul can call baptism a "washing of regeneration." ... And the oral gospel "is the power of God for salvation to every one who has faith."[19]

Coupled with the emphasis on the feelings of the sanctified heart as an assurance for salvation, Pietism in general and Methodism in particular stressed a brand of holiness that strove for moral perfection. In Methodist teaching, this stage of "entire sanctification" was reached through a post-conversion experience of great religious trauma and intensity, which was called the "second blessing" of the Spirit.[20] The spotlight in pietistic revivalism had clearly intensified its focus on sanctification, rather than justification.[21]

Pietism still exerts its influence today. Not only in the experience-oriented theology of popular Evangelicalism, but also in the intensely physical manifestations of the Spirit sought in the charismatic movement, we see the direct results of the labors of Spener, Zinzendorf, Wesley and others.

The "missing link" in the journey of holiness religion to the modern American scene is found in the Keswick teachers of late nineteenth century England, who revised Methodistic-Holiness teachings of "the Baptism of the Holy Spirit," or "second blessing" and spoke of repeated emptyings by consecration and "fillings" of the Holy Spirit. They asserted that there are two stages of Christian experience: the "carnal" and the "spiritual." To move from the lower to the higher takes a definite act of faith or "consecration," a distinct crisis experience which they believed was a requirement for being filled with the Spirit. This consecration they termed "absolute surrender" or "yielding," which meant that the self was now dethroned and God was enthroned.[22]

This sketch of Pietism has brought us full circle. For the modern Christian, it is almost *déjà vu* in reverse. The terminology and techniques are the same as we see in modern experience — oriented Evangelicalism; only the names and dates have changed. Journeying into the headwaters of the Evangelicals we have discovered some familiar currents. The key streams in the "born-again" river of twentieth century America can be traced to seventeenth century Pietism and its theological heirs, Methodism and revivalism.

The Fundamentalist/Modernist controversy

If the streams of revivalism flow within the river of Evangelicalism, it would be fair to say that those streams bear the indelible mark of an intense theological turmoil which began in the late nineteenth century, known as the Fundamentalist/Modernist controversy. It would be very difficult to understand the modern Evangelicals without a brief look at this struggle between faith and modern science. On American shores, this struggle began in the latter decades of the nineteenth century.

During the period of reconstruction after the Civil War, the United States had begun to enter a new era of hope and optimism. Industry and technology were benefiting from the rapid discoveries of modern science, and there was a general feeling that America, together with western civilization as a whole, had turned a corner. The tragedy of warfare and bloodshed was behind; ahead lay only the great achievements human ingenuity could devise for the benefit of everyone. Coupled with this belief in the potential of science and industry was a general optimism regarding the human spirit and the nature of man. This was an era of deep romanticism in the arts and literature which focused on the inherent goodness in people.

It wasn't long before the optimism of the age infiltrated the churches. With this world view around them, and with many of the prominent advocates of social optimism in the pews before them, it is not surprising that many of the well-known pulpit orators began to advocate what came to be known as "the new theology." The New Theology was a product of the pulpit rather than the classroom, contrary to Liberalism, its theological descendant. There was now a clear shift in the Christian message. Rather than the atonement of Christ serving as the focal point of the Protestant message, as it had with little variation since the time of the Reformers, the spotlight for preachers of the New Theology was now on a kind of First Article incarnational emphasis. Science is just now giving us real insight into the complexity and beauty of God's world, it was argued. Since Jesus entered this world long ago, by that incarnation he has sanctified the pursuit of scientific discovery and placed his mark of approval on the human spirit. In a word, preachers of this New Theology were more interested in human achievement than in God's salvation.

Besides the inroads made into the churches by the popular preaching of the New Theology, Fundamentalism was also under attack during this time from the lecture halls of its seminaries. Here a new Liberalism was being promulgated, based on the scientific developments in biology and in biblical criticism. Darwin's theories, published originally in his *Origin of the Species* in 1859, appeared to undermine not only the doctrine of special creation, but the very nature of the Bible itself as a book of divine revelation. By the close of the century, his theories had not only gained a following in the seminaries, but in the pulpits of America as well.

Hand in hand with Darwinism, as it was called, went another threat to the fundamental doctrines of Christianity, which became known as "higher criticism." Seminaries at the turn of the century were being increasingly populated by advocates of this new "scientific" approach to the Bible, which had been first introduced in Europe. Now it appeared that the Bible itself was a product of the evolutionary development of certain theologies. Its statements could no longer be taken at face value, but had to undergo the critique of the enlightened scholar to determine what interplay of forces resulted in the words as they were written. Like peeling an onion, the trained expert could eventually peel away enough human additions to arrive at the central core of the text and its message for our time.

The pendulum had swung in the opposite direction from the fire and brimstone revivalism preached by Charles Finney in the earlier part of the nineteenth century. His brand of preaching was now out of fashion, and revivalism re-entered the backwoods, not to emerge again for almost one hundred years.

Not that revivalism was dead; it flourished amid the laity and it was nourished in Bible conferences held throughout the closing decades of the nineteenth and into the twentieth century. It was at one of these Bible conferences at Niagara in 1895 that the stage was set for the greatest doctrinal conflict of modern times.

The "five fundamentals" adopted as a platform for evangelical Pietism at the 1895 conference were: the inerrancy of the Scriptures, the deity of Jesus Christ, the virgin birth, the substitutionary theory of the atonement, and the bodily resurrection of the Lord together with his imminent return.[23] The Fundamentalists launched a concerted effort to obtain control of the leadership of denominations, seminaries, mission societies, etc.

The most visible outcome of this effort was the publication of twelve small, but well-written volumes entitled *The Fundamentals*. Financed by two wealthy laymen over a period of seven years starting in 1909, this series was distributed to every clergyman in the nation. Despite their aggressive campaign, Fundamentalist forces were able to retain noticeable control in only one denomination, the Presbyterian Church. By majority vote, its General Assembly had managed to adopt the five fundamentals, and efforts began to enforce doctrinal discipline against those who would not abide by them. Yet, despite their initial success, Fundamentalists eventually lost their influence in the power structure of American churches. This loss was underlined by the 1929 departure of the great Bible scholar and Fundamentalist champion, J. Gresham Machen, from Princeton Theological Seminary, once a bastion of Old School Presbyterianism.[24]

Fundamentalism had been dealt its death blow in the public eye four years earlier, when a Tennessee school teacher, John Scopes, had been convicted of violating laws enacted against the teaching of the evolutionary theories of Darwin. Though his successful prosecution had been led by the eminent William Jennings Bryan, it was Bryan who was, in effect, convicted by a worldwide press and held up to public scorn and ridicule. As a lasting legacy of the Scopes trial, Fundamentalism was equated in the public eye with blind anti-intellectualism and an unscientific world view.

When Machen finally was forced out of Princeton and founded the Orthodox Presbyterian Church, it looked as though Fundamentalism had been banished forever from the public scene to take up residence in a few schismatic churches and in the backwoods of Appalachia and the South. Little could its sophisticated opponents dream that a Fundamentalist renaissance would take place only forty years later. It would be a Fundamentalism purged of its backward belligerence and clothed with a new sophistication of its own. And it would have a new name of its own choosing: the New Evangelicalism.

The New Evangelicals

Whether or not there is any direct connection between the post World War II period and the rise of the New Evangelicals is difficult to determine. One could speculate that the great increase in the numbers of young parents with children could signal a turn in the direction of tried and true standards and values. In addition, a nation which had undergone the turmoil of war would recognize the need for a religious foundation based on something other than the human spirit. At any rate, the shift from Fundamentalism to Evangelicalism can be traced roughly to the period of 1942 (when the National Association of Evangelicals was founded) to 1960.

After 1960, two groups are identifiable among conservative Protestants: Fundamentalists and New Evangelicals. They are "two camps without definite boundaries," as Bruce Shelley has observed.[25] On the one hand, Fundamentalism has always been noted for a militant stridency, taking its stand for doctrinal integrity on the basis of uncompromising loyalty to the text of the Bible. In contrast, New Evangelicals have a more polished, urbane style. They hold many of the same doctrines as the Fundamentalists, but with more openness toward the viewpoints of their opponents and with much more sensitivity (some would say proclivity) toward the culture.[26]

The doctrinal base of modern Evangelicalism is much broader than that of any of the movements which preceded it. For instance, many wings of Evangelicalism are happy to use higher critical approaches to scriptural interpretation, though their fundamentalist predecessors at the turn of the century regarded this view of the Bible as heresy. Another example of doctrinal diversity within the Evangelical camp is on the subject of eschatology (the end times). Sizeable numbers of Evangelical leaders still hold to the premillennial view of their revivalist forebears — namely, that Jesus will return to set up an earthly kingdom during which there will be a thousand year period of peace and prosperity for the church. Growing numbers of Evangelicals, however, have defected to amillennialism — the view that there will be no thousand year earthly kingdom before or after his return. In so doing they seem to be reflecting the tastes of their constituency: Hal Lindsey's popular premillennialist books[27] no longer arouse the intense excitement they caused fifteen years ago.

Even though modern Evangelicals are more doctrinally diverse than Fundamentalists, it is still possible to define the general theological framework on which Evangelicalism is built. George Marsden lists five doctrinal components in modern Evangelicalism:

> 1. the Reformation doctrine of the final authority of Scripture;

2. the real, historical character of God's saving work recorded in Scripture;
3. eternal salvation only through personal trust in Christ;
4. the importance of evangelism and missions;
5. the importance of a spiritually transformed life.[28]

Judged by these categories, conservative Lutherans have been included by some observers within the ranks of Evangelicalism.[29]

To the naked eye, conservative Lutheranism appears to be a curious abnormality within American Christendom: too liturgical to be truly Evangelical, too fundamentalistic to be "mainline." Certainly there is substantial agreement between Evangelicals and conservative Lutherans in the area of biblical authority and the historicity of the Gospel. Since the time of the Reformation Lutherans have also shown a consistent concern for evangelizing the lost. And every indication is that Lutherans in America are increasingly mission-minded. However, profound differences in the area of conversion and sanctification remain, the very differences that gave rise to this study.

This is not merely a case of parochial jealousy or a clash of traditions. Lutherans and Evangelicals may share a common respect for the authority of the Word of God and a common vocabulary in the proclamation of Christ's atoning work, but they each breathe a different atmosphere. Like Luther and Zwingli before them, they may shake hands but must unhappily conclude that they have a "different spirit." The differences are not incidental to, but rather integral to the gospel: Is salvation God's action or the believer's? That has been the basic issue all along.[30] It continues to be.

No matter how we evaluate the doctrine of the Evangelicals, it is clear that their day in the sun has arrived. 1976 was declared by *Newsweek* magazine as the year of the Evangelicals. Twelve years later, despite the Bakker and Swaggart debacles, the momentum of this movement shows no signs of slowing. Fueled by America's cultural veneer of political and social conservatism, it has shown remarkable tenacity. One reason for its staying power may be the debilitation of its historic enemy, Liberalism.

The bankruptcy of Liberalism

Classic religious Liberalism in the United States is a product of the general optimism of the turn of the century coupled with a disillusionment with the old dogmas, since they appeared to be in conflict with the discoveries of science. Albert Schweitzer, in his 1906 book, *The Quest for the Historical Jesus*, found that applying the new science of higher critical interpretation to the New Testament left the historical Jesus completely inaccessible to the modern Christian. Earlier theologians had traced much of Christian dogma to the accretions of the imaginations of the early church (Ritschl [d. 1889]) or to its interplay with other world religions ("History of Religions" school, ca. 1890). Left with little or no basis for reliable information about its Founder, Christianity was left to concentrate on his ethical teachings. For example, T. H. Huxley said in 1890: "I visualize the days not far hence when faith will be separated from all facts . . . and then faith will go on triumphant forever."[31] Liberals thought they had safeguarded the faith from attack at the hands of reason by divorcing faith from history:

Religion would no longer be seen as dependent on historical or scientific fact susceptible of objective inquiry; religion had to do with the spiritual, with the heart, with religious experience, and with moral sense or moral action — areas not open to scientific investigation. Thus science would have its autonomy, and religion would be beyond its reach.[32]

For a time, the Liberal emphasis on ethics over dogma proved to be quite popular. Its influence can be traced all the way from the early emphasis on the social gospel advocated by its greatest spokesman, Walter Rauschenbusch (d. 1918), to the involvement of Christian activists in the great social upheavals of the Civil Rights and Anti-War Movements of the 1960s.

This kind of "Alice in Wonderland" theology could not survive. Even though the Mad Hatter might claim that words mean whatever he wants them to mean, Liberalism found that approach did not work in theology. Setting out to separate fact from faith, they had come to an impasse. The house they had constructed to protect them from the assault of reason was made of cards. Today, though Liberalism still reigns in many parts of the public media, we are witnessing its collapse under its own weight.

"What the liberal establishment does not yet comprehend," Jeremy Rifkin wrote in 1979, "is the hard, cold reality that American Liberalism has already begun a *permanent* slide into extinction."[33] Arguing that economic upheaval is bringing about a new Protestant reformation, a "conservation ethic," Rifkin has some interesting observations about the decline of Liberalism:

It is important to bear in mind that, within the American experience, both conservative and liberal politi-

41

cal beliefs are children of a common parent, the liberal ethos. Each accepts the notion that individual self-interest and unlimited material growth are the *sine qua non* of human social existence. Both place their total faith in science, technology and capitalism as the ruling deities of the modern world.[34]

As confidence in science and technology diminish, the liberal ethos is gradually losing its monopoly on American thought patterns. What will take its place? Rifkin predicts a resurgence of conservative Calvinism:

America, then, is made up of two cultures which exist in a carefully structured relationship to one another. The Reformation culture of John Calvin remains the basis of the American experience. Its bastardized successor, the liberal ethos, remains superimposed on top but it is continually influenced by the subtle shifts and quiet rumblings of its earlier foundation.[35]

Whether or not Rifkin's theories are correct, he is not the only commentator who has detected the serious erosion of Liberalism as a driving force in American church life. Bloesch writes: "As a spiritual movement within the churches, liberalism is slowly but surely giving way to both classical evangelicalism and fundamentalism."[36] Remember Richard John Neuhaus's wry observation of the predicament of the liberal establishment? " . . . it is the certitudes of Clarence Darrow which now seem pitiably quaint."[37] The defeat of Fundamentalism at the Scopes trial has now been reversed. The disgrace of William Jennings Bryan has been avenged; the great silver tongued orator has had the final say. It took only sixty years for the liberal pendulum to swing into conservatism. American religious Liberalism has collapsed as a viable option.

The Evangelical initiative

Evangelical theology has undertaken a new initiative, turning the corner from its Fundamentalist past. Its efforts are certainly capitalizing on the collapse of the old Liberalism, if not contributing to it. At least four components make up this initiative: Evangelicalism's scholarship, its cultural sensitivity, its use of the media and its popular piety or life style.

Scholarship

In 1960, just as the New Evangelical movement was beginning to make headway, Harold Ockenga wrote in *Christianity Today*, the foremost Evangelical journal, that three objectives lay before the movement: (1) academic respectability, (2) social involvement and (3) denominational redirection.[38] History has shown at least a measure of success in every one of these areas.

Equipped with credentials from respected academic institutions both at home and abroad, Evangelical scholars began a vigorous critique of neo-orthodoxy, which then held full sway in theological circles. Their efforts in biblical studies have been unexcelled by any other conservative scholars. Twentieth century conservative Lutherans, for example, have proven to be much more adept at systematics than biblical studies. They have relied on Evangelical writers to chart the course through the rough seas of liberal biblical scholarship.[39]

Nevertheless, Evangelical scholarship has not met with universal approval from those within its own ranks. For example, some see its emphasis on an intellectual defense of the faith as extremely dangerous. Reason, they argue, is legitimately used only in dealing with historical data. Faith alone can grasp the revelation God offers us in history. Naming Carl Henry, John W. Montgomery, Norman Giesler and Francis Schaeffer (all cult heroes of New Evangelicals to varying degrees) as offenders, Donald Bloesch, a prominent Evangelical spokesman, questions Evangelicalism's "bent toward rationalism."[40] It remains to be seen whether Evangelicalism will be able to retain its position on the limb of scholarship without sawing itself off the trunk of revelation.

Cultural sensitivity

With impressive energy, Evangelicalism has conducted not only an attack against its liberal Christian peers, but a lively mission to the unbelieving society in which it lives. Here, no doubt influenced by revivalism before it, Evangelicals have made conversion of the lost a prime focus. There is a distinct difference in style, however, between the evangelistic message of Fundamentalism and that of Evangelicalism. Evangelicals tend to be much more in tune with the culture around them than were their Fundamentalist predecessors. They aim to translate the Christian message for the unbelieving public; this translation is to be rendered in the language of contemporary American culture. Bloesch captures the rationale behind Evangelicalism's cultural sensitivity when he writes:

> There cannot be theological points of contact between the gospel and the world, but there must be sociological and cultural points of contact. We must speak the language of our age even while seeking to overthrow its follies and superstitions.[41]

Here most American churches can learn from the Evangelicals. Liberal Christianity has tended to engage in theological discussion with the world, and it has frequently compromised the gospel for the world's sake. At the other extreme are conservative confessional churches, which have tended to create their own culture. In mission outreach, converts have often had to undergo "culture shock" in order to find their way into the mainstream of conservative Lutheran church life.

Evangelicals have shown that they are not only sensitive but also sympathetic to the culture around them. Sensing the needs and moods of society, they have packaged the Christian gospel in ways that appeal to people faced with the complexities of American life in the closing decades of the twentieth century. Here we might mention loneliness, despair and anxiety as examples of the kinds of problems for which Evangelicals have offered the solutions.

It could be asked, however, if the Evangelicals' laudable interest in the culture has not already compromised the gospel. The Evangelical victory is at least partially riding in on the coattails of a general conservative landslide in society. Where does conservative political and economic concern leave off and Evangelicalism begin? " . . . one can ask," Donald Bloesch wrote already in 1973, "whether the evangelical renaissance is rooted in a profound spiritual awakening or in the counter-revolution of middle America against the vagaries of the New Left."[42]

What is needed is a method sensitive to the mood of the culture without compromising the Christian message. Some critics, such as Jeremy Rifkin, believe that the most subjective of the Evangelicals have already gone too far down that path for retreat: "[The charismatic movement's] vertical posture, its elimination of time and space (immediate communication with God), its unity between God and people and its emotional experiential nature all reflect the TV culture (instant, spontaneous, subjective, and emotional)"[43]

Here the real danger is that the medium becomes the message, that the experiential, subjective packaging of this brand of Evangelicalism has taken over the content of the gospel. How ironic it would be if Huxley's prediction nearly a hundred years ago about the separation of fact from faith[44] would come true not within Liberalism, but within the family of revivalism!

It would appear that Evangelicalism's flirtation with the culture has influenced it more than it admits. Its preaching and worship have tended to imitate some of the more spectacular components of our culture:

> What the church does best — preach, worship, and partake of the sacraments — is, however, discounted as ineffectual ritual and not "real" action. Should the church refuse to be cast in the role of hustler, then the para-ecclesiastical storm troopers stream in to bridge the gap. Media blitzes, advertising compaigns, concert circuits, radio and television networks, clubs, camps, conferences. All aspects of American culture are duplicated and supposedly baptized. One feels securely a part of the mainstream.[45]

The Evangelical initiative in the face of the collapse of Liberalism has been vigorous and effective. It contains much to be admired and imitated. Cultural sensitivity serves the outreach of the church much more effectively than cultural isolationism. Caution, however, is called for. The warning signals include an apparent growing social respectability for conservative Christianity. Respectability is one thing; being considered chic is another. Historically since the time of Constantine, whenever the church has allied itself too closely with the cultural establishment, it has become corrupt and its gospel has been secularized.

Aggressive use of media

One of the most visible characteristics of the Evangelical initiative has been its utilization of radio and television and, more recently, other forms of communication now available through electronic technology. One of the key avenues of Evangelical outreach has been through what has become known as "Christian music."

> By 1981, contemporary gospel music had become a $100-million-a-year business. . . . gospel had become the fifth-largest-selling category of music — bigger than classical or jazz. In 1983, gospel accounted for 5 percent of the total market in records and tapes, as compared to 4 percent for classical and 2 percent for jazz. Christian radio stations had boomed along with Christian product; more than 300 stations were spinning Christian discs exclusively, and most of the one-in-eight stations in the country classified as religious broadcasters were airing gospel on a regular basis.[46]

The Christian music industry has had a noticeable effect on the airwaves; there is hardly a community in the country that does not have its own local "Christian radio." Already in 1979 one out of every seven radio stations in the nation was religiously oriented and every seven days a new one was being established. Twenty percent of the television viewing market was being reached by Christian TV stations that were being established at the rate of one every thirty days.[47]

Here again Evangelicalism has been criticized for its efforts to sell the gospel in packaging attractive to the public. Virginia Owens, for example, has questioned the use of secular advertising techniques in evangelistic outreach through the media:

> The point is to make the picture so appealing that the customer wants to see himself within the frame. Health, wealth, youth (or at least youthful age), sharp clothes, exuberant optimism. Is the product Coca-Cola or Christ? It's hard to tell.[48]

The catechesis of life style

The most startling thing about the New Evangelical initiative is that it has turned out to be much more an experience than a recognizable doctrinal system. The Evangelical doctrinal agenda is much broader and more difficult to define than the specific list of concerns brought forward by Fundamentalism. Not all who classify themselves Evangelical would insist on the inerrancy of the Bible or a specific view of the return of Christ, for example. Yet Evangelicalism is a cohesive whole, a recognizable and important segment within Christendom.

What holds Evangelicalism together is a common form of piety, not a common doctrine. The basis of all Evangelical piety is conversion, understood to be a clearly defined personal experience. A particular vocabulary is used in prayer and conversation which immediately identifies the speaker as Evangelical. Particular styles of music are considered "Christian," and a multi-million dollar book industry has grown up around the Evangelical subculture. Heavy stress is placed on "discipleship," which translates as learning to apply scriptural principles into various circumstances of personal life. Thus there has been a huge growth in Bible seminars, conferences and workshops. Within American Evangelicalism, conferences on life style have replaced catechisms as the chief teaching tool of the church.

> Life style workshops are the means by which we learn how to make the necessary alterations and adjustments. Whatever style one opts for in one's life, there is a seminar somewhere that will show you how to fit it. You can learn how to be a Total Woman or an OK guy. There is prosperity training for the Christian businessman and assertiveness training for the Christian feminist. Cooking for Christians and dieting for Christians. Salvation through solar energy and effective parenthood.[49]

At many Evangelical conferences, the emphasis is clearly on internalizing the faith in an experiential way. Bloesch has deplored Evangelicalism's tendency to substitute process for content:

> It is disconcerting to realize that at so many evangelical conferences and retreats, group dynamics and small group discussion figure more prominently than scholarly lectures. . . . It is not an exaggeration to claim that John Dewey wields greater influence at many such meetings than either Karl Barth or John Calvin.[50]

The teaching of life style instead of doctrine has progressed to the point where many American Protestants know more about the hit charts of Christian

49

popular music than they do about the faith. Thanks to the businesses which have grown up around life style Christianity, Evangelicalism can now offer its faithful a life completely insulated from secular distractions.

> Christians can now spend an entire day within an evangelical context, even as they continue to function in the broader secular culture. In the morning, husband and wife wake up to an evangelical service on their local Christian owned and operated radio station. The husband leaves for work where he will start off his day at a businessman's prayer breakfast. The evangelical wife bustles the children off to their Christian Day School. At midmorning she relaxes in front of the TV set and turns on her favorite Christian soap opera. Later in the afternoon, while the Christian husband is attending a Christian business seminar, and the children are engaged in an after-school Christian sports program, the Christian wife is doing her daily shopping at a Christian store, recommended in her Christian Business Directory. In the evening the Christian family watches the Christian World News on TV and then settles down for dinner. After dinner, the children begin their Christian school assignments. A Christian baby-sitter arrives — she is part of a baby-sitter pool from the local church. After changing into their evening clothes, the Christian wife applies a touch of Christian make-up, and then they're off to a Christian nightclub for some socializing with Christian friends from the local church. They return home later in the evening and catch the last half hour of the '700 Club, the evangelical Johnny Carson Show. The Christian wife ends her day reading a chapter or two from Marabel Morgan's best-selling Christian book, *The Total Woman*. Meanwhile her husband leafs through a copy of *Inspiration* magazine, the evangelical *Newsweek*, before they both retire for the evening.[51]

Whatever else may be said in favor of the environment created for Christians by Evangelicalism, it is fair to say that it has a certain monastic tinge. Perhaps motivated by a laudable desire to let their light shine, the life style advocated by the movement's popular piety tends to direct most of its candlepower inwardly. Intended to be yeast in the world, Evangelicals often only bake their own loaves. Intended to be salt for a world rotting at its core, Evangelical Christians all too frequently concentrate only on decorating the saltcellars.

I would go so far as to suggest that New Evangelical conservatism — which arose in the '70s — is nothing more than a continuation of the '60s liberal mindset: the elevation of self. Now instead of the individual finding fulfillment through social activism, satisfaction is to be found in concentration on emotional balance, adjustment and success, all within a Christian framework.[52]

If my discussion of the initiative undertaken by Evangelicalism has seemed negative, please remember that unsuccessful movements rarely have critics. The fact that many of the criticisms brought forward in this section have come from the Evangelical camp itself speaks well of the potential of the movement. Whether it can retain enough objectivity to keep from putting all of its theological eggs into the basket of the prevailing cultural mood remains to be seen. One day — perhaps soon — our culture will lose its conservative, subjective mood. Evangelicals could end up with an unplanned omelette! The church's message should always be determined by the Scriptures, not by its culture.

We have now completed our expedition into the historical background of modern Evangelicalism. Though selective, our stops along the way have shown one consistent theme: all of the movements which have led to modern Evangelicalism have focused on the renewed Christian life. The situation has, if anything, intensified since Donald Bloesch wrote in 1973 about an Evangelicalism still then called "new":

> [Among the Evangelicals] it is not the justification of the ungodly, which formed the basic motif in the Lutheran Reformation and also in neo-orthodoxy, but the sanctification of the righteous that is given the most attention.[53]

So goes the theory. But can it be substantiated? Does sanctification in fact have the central place in Evangelical Christianity? Is it true that this tends to compromise the gospel? It is time to take a look at just how the evangelical emphasis on sanctification is presented to the Christian reading public.

3

THE CHRISTIAN IN ACTION: SANCTIFICATION IN SELECTED WRITINGS OF CHARLES SWINDOLL

We have already seen that Evangelicals have devoted considerable energy to theological scholarship. Scholarly literature has really taken a back seat to popular literature, however, in putting the Christian world into an Evangelical mold.[1] Evangelical book publishing has become big business, and today's shopper can hardly find a grocery store that hasn't been stocked with an Evangelical book display. The popular writings of the New Evangelicals have been one of the most important ways in which their influence has spread. These books routinely revolve around sanctification. In most, lines are drawn between every day life concerns and the new life of the Spirit. In many, techniques and principles are set forth to guide the believer toward what is said to be fuller Christian life. The formula has worked. Sales have mushroomed and more and more people can be found discussing what they found useful in the latest Christian paperback they have read.

Sales of these books are not limited to Fundamentalists, of course. Increasingly Christians of all denominational backgrounds find themselves attracted to the brand of practical religion they find in the popular writings of the Evangelicals. Gradually the personal spirituality and religious vocabulary of Christians of many confessions are beginning to take on an Evangelical coloring.

What are these books talking about? What makes them so popular? What is their theological content? The answers would depend on which author you looked at, but in order at least to get a handle on these questions I have selected three representative books of one best-selling Evangelical author.

Charles R. ("Chuck") Swindoll is senior pastor of the First Evangelical Free Church in Fullerton, California. A gifted and popular speaker, he is much sought after for conferences and Bible seminars across the nation. His international radio ministry, *Insight for Living*, is aired over thirteen hundred times each day on over 900 stations.[2] A prolific author, he has written over twenty-five books on various aspects of the Christian life. His popular trilogy, *Improving Your Serve, Strengthening Your Grip* and *Dropping Your Guard*, were on and off the religious book bestsellers list for several years. Gleaned from material presented in his widely renowned pulpit ministry, these books represent Swindoll at his best.

In the following pages, I will be analyzing these three books with specific reference to the doctrine of sanctification they teach. In some ways, they resist analysis since they were written for popular consumption, not as textbooks of systematic theology. This very purpose, however, makes them all the more interesting for our study. Here we can see how Evangelical teaching on sanctification is formulated by one writer for Christians living in the real world. In some instances my own summary statements introduce the quotations. Other than that, what you read in this chapter is pure Swindoll. I have tried to be as objective as I can in letting him speak for himself.

The purpose of sanctification

The glory of God[3]

Authentic servanthood is " ... being willing to give it all up to Him, for His glory" (I.S., 35).[4] Obedience " ... pleases and glorifies Him ... " (S.G., 248). In heaven servants do not display the crowns they have earned, they are " ... ascribing worth and honor to the only One deserving of praise — the Lord God!" (I.S., 207)

Obeying the will of God

A real disciple of the Lord " ... comes to that place where no major decision is made without a serious consideration of the question, 'What would the Lord want me to do?' as opposed to, 'How will this benefit me?' " (S.G., 117) In doing mission work, "The greatest confirmation that one needs is not the tangible results of one's labors, but the inner assurance he or she is in the nucleus of God's will" (S.G., 191).

The imitation of Jesus

Jesus came to serve, and to give his life as a ransom for many. "He came to serve and to give. It makes sense, then, to say that God desires the same for us" (I.S., 18). If we are injured by others in our life of service, "it's all part of the humbling process God uses in shaping our lives 'to bear the family likeness of His Son' [Rom. 8:29, Phillips]" (I.S., 180).

The reception of spiritual blessings

The Christian learns thankfulness through servanthood. " . . . when you and I take the role of a servant, there is *the joyful realization that a thankful spirit is being stimulated*" [italics his] (I.S., 202). Developing deeper, closer, more loving and open relationships with others " . . . may be the central catalyst God would use to bring a fresh touch of His Spirit back into your church and its congregation" (D.G., 191). Heaven awaits those who live their lives as dedicated servants: "To those who serve, to those who stand where Jesus Christ once stood many, many years ago, He promises a reward" (I.S., 209).

Victory

The wicked may seem to come out ahead of the Christian servant. "The ultimate victory will *not* be won by the wicked. The gentle will win" (I.S., 106). "Those who are gentle . . . will win out" (I.S., 108).

Example to fellow Christians

When others follow Swindoll's example of openness and vulnerability, they will discover they cannot live any other way. "Living without masks is addictive. It's also terribly contagious" (D.G., 207).

Growth in faith

Growth in discipleship is more important than attending large church meetings and evangelistic crusades. Discipleship " ... helps personalize one's faith, moving people out of the spectator realm and onto the playing field" (S.G., 108). The background or social standing of the person who pursues godliness does not matter. " ... what *does* matter is the individual's inner craving to know God, listen to Him, and walk humbly with Him" (S.G., 197). The Bible was given to show us the way to full spiritual maturity:

> I have been absorbing the teachings of Scripture every year of my adult life since the late 1950s, and I have been communicating those principles every week, often several times a week, since that time. The lens through which I filter my perceptions and my convictions is, therefore, the Bible. Its relevance and its wisdom will be seen as each chapter of this book develops. Hopefully, you will discover that God's Word is both timely and true, able to release you from the thick cocoon of fear and give you wings to fly free of all masks. Contrary to popular opinion, God gave us His Book to release us to reach our full potential ... not to push us into a corner and watch us squirm! (D.G., 12)

Thus the Bible is fundamentally a collection of principles geared to help us in right living and to reach our full potential as servants of God. Where does the gospel fit in?

The gospel

Freedom from the power of sin

> We have been freed. Gloriously freed! Before salvation we had no hope. We were victims of all those impulses and defenses within us. But at the cross, our

Savior and Lord defeated the enemy. He said, "It is finished," *and it was*! No longer does sin reign as victor. (I.S., 89)

The possibility of forgiveness

When the penalty of our sin was paid in full by Jesus Christ on the cross, God's wrath was expressed against Him — the One who took our place. God was therefore satisfied in the epochal sacrifice . . . allowing all who would turn, in faith, to the Son of God to be totally, once-for-all, forgiven. Christ's blood washed away our sin. And from the moment we believe on Him, we stand forgiven, relieved of guilt, before a satisfied God, freeing Him to shower upon us His grace and love. (I.S., 57)

Obstacle to spiritual growth

When the Christian uses the gospel as an excuse for his sin, it stifles spiritual maturation.

We can even defend our life style by a rather slick system of theological accommodation. . . . All it takes is a little Scripture twisting and a fairly well-oiled system of rationalization and we are off and running. Two results begin to transpire: (1) all our desires (no matter how wrong) are fulfilled, and (2) all our guilt (no matter how justified) is erased. And if anybody attempts to call us into account, label them a legalist and plow right on! It also helps us to talk a lot about grace, forgiveness, mercy, and the old nobody's-perfect song.

Paul rejected that stuff entirely. He refused to be sucked into such a system of rationalization. He panted after God. He thirsted deep within his soul for the truth of God so he might live it. He longed to take God seriously. (S.G., 198)

Power to overcome trials

Relating a hymn sung by Joni Eareckson, para-lyzed Christian author who did not give up in spite of obstacles: "Though Satan should buffet, tho' trials should come, Let this blest assurance control, That Christ has regarded my helpless estate, And hath shed His own blood for my soul" (S.G., 218).

Removal of offense

God requires us to make amends to those we have offended. When David sought God's forgive-ness for his adultery, " . . . Uriah was not there to hear his confession. . . . But David was not alone. . . . And when the broken king poured out his soul, 'I have sinned . . . , ' Nathan followed quickly with these affirming words: 'The Lord also has taken away your sin; you shall not die' (2 Sam. 12:13)" (I.S., 63).

Mold for the church

It is time the church quit condemning hurting peo-ple. "Long enough have those who need a place of refuge occupied the local bar. It's time we made the church of Jesus Christ — the family of God — a place of refuge. It's time we held high the lamp of forgive-ness, the torch of grace" (D.G., 140).

The bond of unity in the church

We are all one in the body of Christ. "He, alone, brings the body together. As the Head, He is in charge of all the body members. He, therefore, makes the blend of unity possible" (D.G., 81).

The function of the human will in faith

Conversion

The human will is capable of making the decision of faith. "Choosing to let Christ come into your life is not insignificant. . . . Give some serious thought to turning your life over to Christ" (D.G., 166). " . . . Jesus Christ is ready to receive whomever may come to Him by faith" (S.G., 234). Forgiveness is available to " . . . all who would turn, in faith, to the Son of God . . . " (I.S., 57). Personal testimony is a matter of sharing the experience of conversion (S.G., 230).

Assurance

The decision of faith results in the assurance of God's mercy. "The person with a servant's heart . . . is promised a place in Christ's kingdom" (I.S., 102). " . . . this reward [the imperishable crown] will be awarded those believers who consistently bring the flesh under the Holy Spirit's control, refusing to be enslaved by their sinful nature" (I.S., 205).

Maintain a relationship with God

By deciding to obey the principles God has set forth in His Word, the believer experiences God's continuing love and blessing. "God honors a spirit of unity among His people" (D.G., 83). "To maintain a close connection with our Lord, we think of Him as we make our plans, we pray, we explore the rich treasures of His Word" (S.G., 31). By following the principles he has outlined, Swindoll hopes that Jesus Christ may be "more real" to his readers (S.G., 269).

Resisting temptation

Christ assists the human will to resist temptation. "In Christ, through Christ, because of Christ, we have all the internal equipment necessary to maintain moral purity" (S.G., 57). " . . . we need the power of God to walk in purity. The good news is this: *We have it!*" (S.G., 59)

The natural mind, however, resists the principles God wants to convey to us. "As the Spirit of God attempts to communicate His truth to us (biblical information on servanthood, for example), He runs up against our 'wall,' our overall mental attitude, our natural mind-set" (I.S., 87). "As the principles of the Scripture are declared, our natural, unrenewed minds not only resist them, they ask, 'Who needs that?' or 'I've gotten along pretty good up 'til now' " (I.S., 89).

The demands of the new life often lead to apostasy. ". . . discipleship never fails to thin the ranks" (S.G. 118).

Sinful desires must be rooted out by prayer. " 'Please root from my heart all those things which I have cherished so long and which have become a very part of my living self, so that Thou mayest enter and dwell there without a rival' " (S.G., 120).

Requesting Christ to change our lives

There is a difference between being a Christian and being a disciple (S.G., 113). "I was a Christian, but certainly *not* a disciple" (S.G., 124). Christians must therefore consciously decide to serve the Lord fully.

> . . . if you've decided not to let Christ get much beyond the front door of your heart, you may feel that I'm getting into areas that are none of my business. But if

> you are sincerely hungry for maturity — if you are
> sick and tired of being a spectator and you long to let
> Christ invade every room of your life, rearranging
> the furniture of your mind and getting control of the
> appetites of your heart — you are obviously ready to
> dig deeper. (D.G., 26)

Christ's control over our lives hinges on our decision. "I want to encourage you to make that . . . commitment, starting today. Yes, you can! The only thing standing in your way is that decision to turn your life over to Him" (S.G., 143). "God promises that He will pour His power into us (Phil. 4:13) and supply all we need if we will simply operate under His full control" (I.S., 92). "Nothing is too hard for the Lord. No one is beyond hope. *It is never too late to start doing what is right*" (S.G., 203).

God chastises the stubborn will. He is looking for surrender to His divine authority. " 'When God wants to do an impossible task, He takes an impossible person and crushes him.' With one word, I close —Surrender" (S.G., 250).

The decision of faith is a prerequisite to the committed life. "Not until we fully accept *and appropriate* God's infinite and complete forgiveness on our behalf can we carry out the things I mention in the rest of this chapter" (I.S., 58).

The renewal of the mind is the power for change in the life of the Christian. "It all begins in *the mind.* Let me repeat it one more time. Thinking right always precedes acting right" (I.S., 94).

Changing our own lives

The sanctified will of the Christian is able to take concrete steps for positive change. It is able to seek the assistance of the Holy Spirit. "I would like you to operate on yourself as you read this chapter. Not physically, of course, but spiritually. . . . I invite you to allow the Spirit of God to assist you, handing you the only instrument you need to do soul surgery —the germ-free scalpel of Scripture" (S.G., 88). "You have the scalpel in your hand. Self-examination is now up to you" (S.G., 105).

The Christian can change his motivation. "Those who wish to be His disciples replace their selfish goals and desires with God's desire for them" (S.G., 116).

The function of the human will in works

The Christian must deny self

God-pleasing works begin with a denial of the sinful self. "Those who wish to be His disciples replace their selfish goals and desires with God's desire for them" (S.G., 116). "First, those who desire to follow Him closely must come to terms with *self-denial*. And second, this decision to give ourselves to others (taking up our cross) has to be a *daily* matter" (I.S., 48). "Becoming a *giving* person sounds exciting. But it costs something. It will demand change, and no significant change ever got started without motivation and zeal" (I.S., 51).

To be a true servant of God, it takes genuine humility. " . . . let me challenge you to become 'pure in heart.' Think about what it would mean, what changes you would have to make, what habits you'd have to break . . . most of all, what masks you'd have to peel off" (I.S., 116). We may be considered weak by others (D.G., 20). "Strength comes by being close, in touch, unmasked, and available to one another much more than by being big" (D.G., 54).

The Christian seeks a total commitment

The goal in our life of service is complete control by Christ. "I opened each door of my inner house to let Christ in, room after room after room" (S.G., 124). " . . . let Christ invade every room of your life . . . " (D.G., 26). " . . . make sure that the Lord your God is the heart and center of your family!" (S.G., 257) This commitment is based on a deep inner need. " . . . the godly individual hungers and thirsts after God" (S.G., 196).

Total Christian commitment is based not on the gospel, but on effective communication of the principles for living contained in the Bible.

> A 'new' Reformation is in order, in my opinion. Christians in the last two decades of the twentieth century need a fresh, vital word for our times. Not further revelation. Not more doctrines. Not even a new system of theology, necessarily. What we need is a message, securely riveted to scriptural foundations, that has a ring of relevance to it — and authentic reality about it. Ancient truth in today's talk. In Luther's day that meant one thing — the need for clarification to dispel ignorance. *Today* it means another — a new style of communication to dispel indifference. (S.G., 268)

God requries good works

God is just as concerned about our life of service as he is about the message of his word. "Unguarded, open relationships within the body of Christ are just as important as the nourishing, accurate dispensing of scriptural truth. We need both" (D.G., 159). "[God] . . . holds us accountable for the way we live" (D.G., 177).

God rewards good works

The Christian may expect to receive benefits in heaven because of his service to God in this life. "Stay on the scaffold [of suffering] . . . trust your heavenly Father to keep His promise regarding your inheritance. It is you who will be blessed" (I.S., 106). "The crown of righteousness will be awarded those who live each day, loving and anticipating Christ's imminent return . . . " (I.S., 206). "This crown [of life] is not promised simply to those who endure suffering and trials . . . but to those who endure their trials, loving the Savior all the way!" (I.S., 206). "Those under-shepherds who fulfill these qualifications (willingness, sacrificial dedication, humility, an exemplary life) will receive this crown of glory" (I.S., 206).

God also promises rewards in this life to those who follow His will. "These traits [in the sermon on the mount] open the door to inner happiness" (I.S., 99). "Obedience results in ultimate happiness" (I.S., 173). " . . . there are few things quite as contagious as authentic, spontaneous, unguarded love in action" (D.G., 47).

The Christian seeks to please God

God is looking for people responsive to His activity in the world; through them He is able to do His will. "Those who stand united become an invincible force through whom God does His greatest work. The secret, remember, is closed ranks and open relationships" (D.G., 87).

Doing God's will is more a matter of the will than emotions. " . . . we can change our feelings with our will only to a certain degree, whereas our behavior is under the complete and maximum control of our will" (D.G., 163).[5] " . . . messages which simply arouse a lot of emotion aren't nearly as vital as those directed to the will" (D.G., 164).

Christians have the will to please God. "Deep down inside Christians I know is a deep-seated desire to release instead of keep . . . to give instead of grab" (I.S., 52). "We Christians have the God-given ability to put our minds on those things that build up, strengthen, encourage, and help ourselves and others" (S.G., 209).

Right attitudes lead to right actions

The place to begin in the Christian life is with God-pleasing attitudes. "Living differently begins with thinking differently" (I.S., 85). "Willingness must precede involvement [in serving others]" (I.S., 172). " . . . the right attitude choice can literally transform our circumstance, no matter how black and hopeless it may appear" (S.G., 215). "People don't live pure lives due to warnings and threats. These things must come from the heart as a result of right choices" (D.G., 161). "This [the cultivation of deeper relationships] takes time, effort, and a spirit of willingness" (D.G., 48). "I want you to give serious thought to staying out of moth balls. Really, the choice is yours" (S.G., 140). "As your friend, let me urge you to take charge of your mind and emotions today. . . . Yes, you *can* if you *will*" (S.G., 217f).

Pledges of commitment precede action. [In the case of the people of Israel in Joshua 1:] "Within their response are promises of cooperation ('we will do'), availability ('we will go'), commitment ('we will obey'), loyalty ('anyone who rebels . . . shall be put to death'), and encouragement ('be strong and courageous')" (D.G., 83).

The Bible is the Christian's guide

The life of service is a matter of faithfulness to the commands of Christ. " . . . He told us to serve and to give. In those words He built a case for unselfish living" (I.S., 35).

The principles that govern the Christian life are derived from the Scriptures. "Each chapter [of Swindoll's book] deals with a different essential that will, if applied in a personal manner, increase your confidence and your ability to cope with current crises, because it rests on the bedrock of inspired revelation, the Holy Bible" (S.G., 14). "Let's make the Bible our foundation in the '80s. And as we apply its insights and guidelines, let's also cultivate a style that is authentic" (S.G., 23).

God becomes real through works of love

Practicing the principles of God's will helps others see him in action. "As we begin to do this [live from authentic Christian commitment], Christianity becomes something that is absorbed, not just worn. It is more than believed; it is incarnated" (S.G., 27). "The full recovery of a brother or sister in God's family often depends on our willingness to step in and assist the person to face and admit the truth, then, hopefully, reach full repentance" (D.G., 111).

The proclamation of the church must be assisted by its actions. "How about your church? Given to be a lighthouse, a place of hope and refuge, is it accomplishing the ultimate objective? Are hurting people really able to be at home there? Can brokenness and pain be admitted?" (D.G., 54)

Implications of Reformed theology for the new life

God's sovereign reign

The Christian may be confident that everything that happens in his life is divinely ordained.

> Nothing touches me that has not passed through the hands of my heavenly Father. Nothing. Whatever occurs [including suffering], God has sovereignly surveyed and approved. We may not know why (we may *never* know why), but we do know our pain is no accident to Him who guides our lives. He is, in no way, surprised by it all. Before it ever touches us, it passes through Him. (I.S., 189)

The idea that God is in absolute control of life can comfort the Christian. "If the aimlessness of the eighties is starting to loosen your confidence in God's sovereign control, this book will help strengthen your grip" (S.G., 15). "Isaiah saw [in a time of great personal turmoil] no confused or anxious deity, but One who sat in sovereign, calm control with full perspective and in absolute authority" (S.G., 185).

The sovereignty of God may terrify us because of our sin. "Isaiah is frightened, beaten, and broken. Not only does he see the Lord sovereign, high and exalted, ... he also hears that God is infinitely holy. And in contrast to his own sinfulness and depravity, he feels doomed ... beaten" (S.G., 186).

God's covenant

If the Christian acts in a God-pleasing way, God will bless him.

> A family gets started on the right foot when Jesus Christ is in each life (husband and wife are both

born again), and when the lengthening shadow of His Lordship pervades that relationship. When a couple makes Christ a vital part of their life, in the terms of the psalm, that's when 'the Lord builds the house,' that's when he 'guards the city.' (S.G., 257f)

"It [God-pleasing closeness] may be the central catalyst God would use to bring a fresh touch of His Spirit back into your church and its congregation" (D.G., 191).

The Christian must act in response to the covenantal promises of God in his Word. "He wants you to know the joy of living an unmasked life. His Book, the Bible, is full of verses and principles that promise you His commitment" (D.G., 39).

The narratives of scripture elucidate God's covenantal response to service that pleases him. "As we travel through the pages of ancient history, we find ample evidence that God honors a spirit of unity among His people" (D.G., 83).

The sacraments

Sacraments are to be understood as divinely-prescribed commands through which Christians respond to him. "This verse [Acts 2:42] says they devoted themselves to the instruction of the apostles, to the ordinances, to prayer, *and* to fellowship" (S.G., 33).

Baptism is a public acknowledgment of a prior faith commitment.

> The African gentleman [in Acts 8] suggested that he be baptized. Wisely, Philip put first things first. With decisive discernment, Philip explained that faith in Jesus *precedes* baptism. That did it! The man believed and was *then* baptized. No ifs, ands, or buts. *First* there was an acceptance of the message and *after that* there was a public acknowledgment of his faith as he submitted to baptism. (S.G., 234)

69

The law

The law of God exercises a purifying effect in the life of the Christian. " ... just as the national body of Israel could not remain strong and healthy unless Canaanite life style was removed, so it is in the body of Christ" (D.G., 152).

God must sometimes first crush the Christian to make him productive. "Some never learn to 'master it' [rebellion] and therefore spend their lives 'under the smarting rod of God,' as the old Puritans used to say" (S.G., 250).

The law of God has the power to change lives. " ... when truth makes an impact on the will, lives begin to change" (D.G., 164).

Success in the Christian life

Christians face sorrows

Being a Christian is no insurance against affliction. "Servants, no matter how useful, godly, unselfish, and admirable, are every bit as human and subject to the perils of life as any other person on earth" (I.S., 142). Churches need a "circle of shelter" for the hurting (D.G., 134).

> Stop and think. Where does a guy go when the bottom drops out? To whom do we Christians turn when stuff that's embarrassing or a little scandalous happens? Who cares enough to listen when we cry? Who affirms us when we feel rotten? Who will close their mouths and open their hearts? And, even though we deserve a swift kick in the pants, who will embrace us with understanding and give us time to heal without quoting verses? Without giving us a cassette tape of some sermon to listen to? Without telling a bunch of other Christians so they can 'pray more intelligently'? (D.G., 128)

> Surrounded by numerous religious types to whom
> everything is "fantastic," "super," and "incredible,"
> let's work hard at being real. This means we are free
> to question, to admit failure or weakness, to confess
> wrong, to declare the truth. When a person is authen-
> tic, he or she does not have to win or always be in the
> top ten or make a big impression or look super-duper
> pious. (S.G., 22)

The Christian life is lived in the real world under the cross. "It is *we* who have hauled His cross out of sight. It is *we* who have left the impression that it belongs only in the sophisticated, cloistered halls of a seminary or beautified beneath the soft shadows of stained glass and cold marble statues" (S.G., 26). "Unlike the shallow, 'whatever you like is fine' kind of accommodating Christianity being marketed to-day by smooth-talking pushers of religious mediocri-ty, Jesus was ever firm and strong on the cost of discipleship" (S.G., 121).

The reality of sin

The immensity of the love of Christ points out the immensity of our sin. "If we are honest, when we measure ourselves by the life of our Lord who humbled Himself even to death on a cross, we cannot but be overwhelmed with the tawdriness and shabbiness, and even the vileness, of our hearts" (I.S., 149).[6]

Leadership style in the church

Leaders are to build up Christ, not their own repu-tation. "When people follow image-conscious leaders, the leader is exalted. He is placed on a pedestal and ultimately takes the place of the head of the church" (I.S., 25).

> . . . recently I received in my daily stack of mail a
> multicolored brochure advertising and announcing a
> series of lectures to be delivered in Los Angeles by a
> man (a Christian "superstar") who has traveled
> widely, whose name is familiar to most folks in the
> family of God. I must confess I lifted my eyebrows
> with surprise when I read these words written in that
> brochure describing the man:
> A *phenomenal individual* . . .
> *In great demand around the world* . . .
> *Today's most sought-after speaker*!
> That's a far cry from the way Jesus Christ described
> Himself. (I.S., 161f).

Discipleship training can become manipulation
when it demands blind obedience of the leader.

> Any ministry that requires blind loyalty and unques-
> tioning obedience is suspect. Not all gurus are in the
> eastern religions, you know. Some discipleship min-
> istries, quite frankly, come dangerously near this
> point. Now I am not discrediting all discipleship pro-
> grams! . . . My main concern is the abuse of power,
> over-accountability that uses intimidation, fear, and
> guilt to promote authoritarianism. (I.S., 83)

The "how-tos" of sanctification

One of the recurring themes of Chuck Swindoll's
theology of sanctification is a stress on scriptural
principles upon which to base Christian life and action. In each of the three books in our study, considerable space is devoted to how people in the Bible
responded to various circumstances. In connection
with these examples, biblical principles, both positive and negative, are deduced for a Christian's application.

The complexities of modern life, in Swindoll's
opinion, call for an approach to the Christian faith

that is down to earth, clearly communicated, and (above all) eminently practical. The Bible must be studied with an eye toward applying "its insights and guidelines" (S.G., 23). "(God's) Book, the Bible, is full of verses and principles that promise you His commitment" (D.G., 39).

The Old Testament can be viewed not only as salvation history, but as the source of principles to be applied in today's church: "Our goal is to gain insight and reproof as God teaches us from these Old Testament scriptures" (D.G., 105). " . . . just as the national body of Israel could not remain strong and healthy unless Canaanite life style was removed, so it is in the body of Christ" (D.G., 152). In the sermon on the mount, Jesus gives us an example of this kind of teaching: " . . . the most comprehensive delineation in all the New Testament of the Christian counterculture . . . " (I.S., 98).

Thanks to the Reformation's emphasis on the scriptural themes of salvation, the facts of God's saving action in Christ are widely known. A modern reformation is needed. Christian people today have a need to hear God's prescribed principles for living clearly elucidated to move them from apathy into action.

> A "new" Reformation is in order, in my opinion. Christians in the last two decades of the twentieth century need a fresh, vital word for our times. Not further revelation. Not more doctrines. Not even a new system of theology, necessarily. What we need is a message, securely riveted to scriptural foundations, that has a ring of relevance to it — an authentic reality about it. Ancient truth in today's talk. In Luther's day that meant one thing — the need for clarification to dispel ignorance. *Today* it means

another — a new style of communication to dispel indifference. (S.G., 268)

Swindoll's view is that the Bible is God's communication of not only a message of salvation, but also principles for living. As people begin to understand and apply these principles in their lives, they are brought into a deeper awareness of God's presence in their lives. The crucial need of the church today is to communicate these principles more clearly and effectively. The result of such communication could be nothing short of revolutionary:

It is my wish that more and more of God's people would become a part of this "new" Reformation — committed to communicating divine revelation so clearly that the public is stunned to realize how eternally relevant God and His Word really are. (S.G., 269)

How to give

To be a servant, we must first learn to give. 2 Corinthians 8 shows us that we should give "anonymously, generously, voluntarily, and personally" (I.S., 43ff).

How to forgive

When we have wronged someone else, Matthew 5:23,24 tells us to do four things: "1. Stop 'leave your offering there... ' 2. Go 'go your way... ' 3. Reconcile ' ... first be reconciled... ' 4. Return ' ... then come and present your offering ... ' " (I.S., 60).

The way to implement forgiveness in our lives is: "First, focus fully on God's forgiveness of you. ... Next, deal directly and honestly with any resentment you currently hold against anyone" (I.S., 67f).

How to forget

In Philippians 3 we find three principles for forgetting the wrongs committed against us: "vulnerability" ('I have not arrived.') "humility" ('I forget what is behind.') "determination" ('I move on to what is ahead.') (I.S., 74ff).

How to be a peacemaker

In the book of Proverbs, God tells us the essential qualities of peacemakers: "They build up. (Prov. 14:1)... They watch their tongues... (Prov. 16:24)... They are slow to anger. (Prov. 15:18) ... They are humble and trusting. (Prov. 28:25)" (I.S., 119).

The perils of servanthood

In the example of Gehazi, Elisha's servant, we find four perils to avoid in striving to be a Christian servant:

> The Peril of Overprotection and Possessiveness (2 Kings 4:29-37)
> The Peril of Feeling Used and Unappreciated (2 Kings 4:38-41)
> The Peril of Disrespect and Resentment (2 Kings 5:14-24)
> The Peril of Hidden Greed (2 Kings 5:25-27) [I.S., 145ff]

How to be obedient

In Christ's model and command, we find three specific principles for obedience in the Christian life: "1. Obedience means personal involvement (John 13:14) ... 2. Obedience requires Christlike unselfishness (John 13:15) ... 3. Obedience results in ultimate happiness. (John 13:17)" (I.S., 172f).

How to cope with suffering

When afflicted with the consequences of living the new life in Christ, remember these two personal truths: "Nothing touches me that has not passed through the hands of my heavenly Father. Nothing. . . . Everything I endure is designed to prepare me for serving others more effectively. Everything" (I.S., 189).

The promise of reward

God promises rewards to those who serve him out of faith. On the basis of 1 Corinthians 3:10-14, the following principles governing rewards can be gleaned: "1. Most rewards are received in heaven, not on earth. . . . 2. All rewards are based on quality, not quantity. . . . 3. No reward that is postponed will be forgotten" (I.S., 195).

The five crowns

The New Testament mentions five eternal crowns set aside for God's servants: "1. The Imperishable Crown (1 Cor. 9:24-27) . . . 2. The Crown of Exultation (Phil. 4:1; 1 Thess. 2:19,20) . . . 3. The Crown of Righteousness (2 Tim. 4:7,8) . . . 4. The Crown of Life (James 1:12) . . . 5. The Crown of Glory (1 Pet. 5:1-4)" (I.S., 205f).

Four priorities for living

To be the most effective we possibly can in our Christian life, it is necessary to follow these essential priorities: "Be Biblical [1 Thess. 2:2-4] . . . Be Authentic [1 Thess. 2:5,6] . . . Be Gracious [1 Thess. 2:7-11] . . . Be Relevant [1 Thess. 2:12,13]" (S.G., 19ff).

How to practice encouragement

There is no better way to stimulate fellow Christians to greater growth than to give them encouragement. " ... when we encourage others, we come as close to the work of the Holy Spirit as anything we can do in God's family" (S.G., 48). Some ways to practice encouragement of others are: observe their admirable qualities and compliment them, send notes and give gifts, phone people with appreciation, express appreciation for a job well done, be supportive in time of need (S.G., 52).

How to control the body

The Bible offers us the following principles for maintaining moral purity:

> We are to present our bodies as living sacrifices to God (Rom. 12:1). We are instructed *not* to yield any part of our bodies as instruments of unrighteousness to sin (Rom. 6:12,13). Our bodies are actually "members of Christ"; they belong to Him (1 Cor. 6:15).
> Our bodies are "temples" literally inhabited by the Holy Spirit (1 Cor. 6:19). We are therefore expected to "glorify God" in our bodies (1 Cor. 6:20). We are to become students of our bodies, knowing how to control them in honor (1 Thess. 4:4). (S.G., 61)

How to handle money

Those who are not rich are reminded in 1 Timothy 6:6-8 to practice godliness plus contentment (S.G., 74). Those who want to become rich are warned in 1 Timothy 6:9,10 that "materialism is a killer; at best, a crippler" (S.G., 80). Those who are rich are instructed in 1 Timothy 6:17-19 not to be conceited, to avoid trusting in their wealth, and to be generous (S.G., 81ff.).

Biblical patterns for the Christian life

Many principles for modern Christian living can be learned from the example of people in the Bible:

Person(s)	Subject	Reference
Daniel	Integrity	(S.G., 91ff)
Caleb	Aging	(S.G., 134ff)
Isaiah	Missions	(S.G., 183ff)
Philip	Witnessing	(S.G., 227ff)
Saul	Rebellion	(S.G., 242ff)
Hebrews	Assimilation	(D.G., 67ff)
Hebrews	Refuge	(D.G., 132ff)
Joshua	Obedience	(D.G., 146ff)

How to be a disciple

In order to be an effective disciple, we must spend time with Jesus as his first followers did. "They watched Him, asked Him questions, listened as He taught, caught His vision, absorbed His ideas and philosophy. That's what Mark means when he says they were 'with Him' " (S.G., 111).

How to pray effectively

Jesus offers three principles for "a satisfying and God-honoring prayer life" (S.G., 153).

1. Don't be hypocritical. (Matt. 6:1,2,5,16)
2. Don't use a lot of repetition. (Matt. 6:7,8)
3. Don't harbor anything against another. (Matt. 6:14,15) [S.G., 153ff]

How to have leisure

Since God's Word tells us that we are to imitate him (Ephesians 5:1), the best way to handle leisure is to practice what we see God doing in Genesis: "He creates [Genesis 1 & 2], He communicates [Genesis

1:26-30], He rests [Genesis 2:1-3], He relates [Genesis 2:21,22]" (S.G., 165ff.).

How to change our attitudes

Christians are told to take charge of their own minds. "We Christians have the God-given ability to put our minds on those things that build up, strengthen, encourage, and help ourselves and others. 'Do that!' commands the Lord" (S.G., 209). Godly attitudes include: unselfish humility [Philippians 2:3,4], positive encouragement [Philippians 2:14], genuine joy [Philippians 4:1,4-7] (S.G., 209ff).

How to get closer to others

Since isolation is destructive to the human personality, we need to cultivate closer relationships. "First, there must be an admission of need for others. . . . Second, there must be the cultivation of deeper relationships. . . . Third, there must be a firm commitment to assimilation" (D.G., 48f).

Christians must be on the alert for four dangers in the process of building group unity: "1. Falling more in love with the leader than with the Lord. 2. Fixing our eyes on our immediate convenience instead of our ultimate objective. 3. Assuming that size means strength. . . . 4. Living in the glow of yesterday instead of the challenge of tomorrow" (D.G., 50ff).

How to build unity

Taking as our example the teamwork practiced by ancient Israel in the conquest of Jericho under Joshua, we can see two suggestions for practical application. "1. The pursuit of unity is hard work, but it's worth it. . . . 2. The place of humility is of highest value, but it's rarely seen" (D.G., 93).

How to love

In 1 Corinthians 13, we can see how God instructs his people in how to express his love to one another. This chapter could be summarized in the "ABCs of Love":

> I *a*ccept you as you are.
>> I *b*elieve you are valuable.
>>> I *c*are when you hurt.
>>>> I *d*esire only what is best for you.
>>>>> I *e*rase all offenses. (D.G., 122)

How to build a caring church

Churches need to change their guarded atmosphere in order for Christians to be able to help one another deal meaningfully with their hurts and burdens.

> Churches need to be less like national shrines and more like local bars . . . less like untouchable cathedrals and more like well-used hospitals, places to bleed in rather than monuments to look at . . . places where you can take your mask off and let your hair down . . . places where you can have your wounds dressed. (D.G., 127) Christianity may be "like a mighty army," but we often handle our troops in a weird way. We're the only outfit I've ever heard of who shoots their wounded. (D.G., 129)

How to change our lives

In the example of Israel under Joshua in Joshua 23, God deals with changing sinful habits in the following concrete ways: "First, he talks about their *attitude.* 'Be very firm' [23:6] . . . Second, he mentions their *actions.* [23:7] . . . Third, he mentions their *alternative* [23:8]" (D.G., 147).

How to lead people

Directive methods are not helpful in molding Christian lives. "Uptight, intense, superdefensive, easily threatened leaders do not spawn congregations of close, caring, relaxed, accepting, completely human, and believable relationships" (D.G., 196).

> People respond much better to personal models than to verbal demands. They are motivated much more by the Joshua method of leadership ("as for me and my house, we will serve the Lord, but you must choose for yourself") than by the rip-snorting, smoke-and-fire screams and threats of the uptight types. It's been my observation in recent years (I learned this *so* late!) that most Christians really don't want to live mediocre lives, but neither do they desire to be driven like cattle. Folks respond more like sheep than steers. (D.G., 161)

How to develop accountability

When people are accountable to others, their church helps them live more effective Christian lives. "We are not islands of independence, living lives free of one another. We are made to relate, to blend into one another, to touch one another, to answer to one another" (D.G., 178).

The book of Proverbs makes the value of accountability clear: "1. By being accountable, we are less likely to stumble into a trap. . . . 2. By being accountable, we don't get away with unwise and sinful actions" (D.G., 180f).

Four practical suggestions for implementing accountability:

> 1. Stop and consider the value of becoming accountable.

The Christian in Action:

2. Ask yourself two questions:
   Why do I remain isolated and unaccountable?
   What if I stay in this condition?
3. Choose at least one other person (preferably two or
   three) with whom you will meet regularly.
4. Develop a relationship that strengthens your grip
   on spiritual things. (D.G. 183f)

How to respond to adversity

In 1 Peter 5:10,11 God promises his blessings when
we face adversity rather than shrink from it. God
will:

Perfect: This term carries with it the idea of repairing
weak or broken parts.

Confirm: To make firm, solid as granite, tough as
fiber, strong as tempered steel.

Strengthen: Take away the flab, replace fragility
with stability.

Establish: This is the idea of laying down a foundation. Suffering drives us back to the bedrock
of our faith. (D.G., 201)

4

LIFE STYLE
CHRISTIANITY
EXAMINED

The mainstream of American culture is much more interested in action than ideas. People today want practical guidelines for life, not complicated discussions of ethical principles. This is the kind of world we live in. It is helpful to know which way the stream is headed before we launch our Christian witness to the world.

I have a question I would like to raise, as gently and winsomely as I can: Is the Evangelical ship perhaps traveling so smoothly and swiftly because it is being swept along by the cultural current?

Of course it is important to understand our world if we want to be faithful to our Lord and effectively proclaim his gospel. What happens, however, when the culture determines what is taught? At worst, it is apostasy. At best, we could call it accommodation. Is it possible that the Evangelical world has crossed the boundary between sensitivity to our world and accommodation to it? Let's examine this issue openly and honestly. I hope you'll find my appraisal both objective and constructive.

It is difficult to analyze a Christian movement that is more style than substance, more form than content. Yet this is precisely what makes Evangelicalism so attractive to modern America. The American marketplace is asking "Will it work? What can you tell me about living my life in today's complex and threatening world? Where in the world is God?" Even from the brief sampling of Swindoll's work I have presented, it is clear that Evangelicals have taken an aggressive lead in providing answers to these questions. This is the Evangelical challenge.

In order to respond properly, it is necessary to take an honest look at this challenge on its own merits. What are its theological foundations? What needs does it perceive in our world? What goals does it hold out for the Christian in this world?

Inner integrity

Swindoll's three books I surveyed were clearly not intended to be a complete summary of the Christian faith. They find their starting point in his concern for the shape of the Christian life in the "aimless eighties."

> We need biblical fixed points to hang onto — firm, solid handles that will help us steer our lives in a meaningful manner. What we really want is something to grab — believable, reliable truth that makes sense for today's generation, essential principles for our aimless world. (S.G., 14)[1]

The following critique is not intended as a comprehensive summary of Swindoll's theology in general, nor his theology of sanctification in particular. These three books have a narrower scope. They represent a pastor's concern for specific issues in contemporary Christian life, presented in a sermonic style. Sermons are not the usual method of summarizing Christian doctrine.

Actually the distinctly popular style of these books makes them even more valuable as samples of the kind of sanctification being advocated by Evangelical spokesmen today. These books were, you will remember, consistent bestsellers in the eighties. Neither author nor reader was looking for a comprehensive theological treatment of sanctification, but the message comes through nevertheless. Comprehensive or not, that message is clear and convincing. The intention is that the reader incorporate that message into his faith and (even more significantly) into his practical piety. "It makes me smile when I think of the benefits that you will begin to enjoy as you lift the truth from these printed pages and transfer it into your talk and your walk" (D.G., 207).

What brand of Christianity is being advocated in these books for day to day piety ("talk and walk")?

Sin

First, it is a brand of Christianity that is free of any pretense of perfectionism. Swindoll makes it clear by his frequent attacks on the shallow claims of "success theology" that perfection is beyond the reach of the Christian in this world.

In comparing the rigid formalism of the church to the open acceptance found in the bar scene, a friend of Swindoll's finds the church sadly wanting.

> The bar flourishes not because most people are alcoholics, but because God has put into the human heart

> the desire to know and be known, to love and be loved, and so many seek a counterfeit at the price of few beers. With all my heart I believe that Christ wants His church to be . . . a fellowship where people can come in and say, "I'm sunk!" "I'm beat!" "I've had it!"[2]

Here we see a distinctly different view of the church from the one held in many parts of American Evangelicalism. Swindoll sees the church as a company of sinners, not perfected saints. No matter what degree of maturity they attain, Christians remain " . . . every bit as human and subject to the perils of life as any other person" (I.S., 142). When so many other authorities are holding out perfectionist goals for the Christian, such a realistic view of man is refreshing.

However, if the Christian presented in these books is not morally perfect, the seriousness of sin is still an open question. I did not find a clear reference to sin and its effect on man and his Creator. Sin is presented rather as a moral imperfection (I.S., 142) which can be considered "vile" in comparison with the immensity of the love of Christ. It can be partially overcome by an act of the will (D.G., 164). Proper choices of the sanctified will, of course, are the focus of these books.

Gospel

Second, if sin is pictured mostly as moral blight, it is not surprising that the gospel gets somewhat of a short shrift. In this view of sanctification, the Christian is left to his own devices. His own sanctified will, not the power of the Holy Spirit, is the motivational power for correct choices in his life. In the three books under study, totaling some 690 pages, there are only six references to the redemption purchased by Christ on the cross. Only one of the six could be called an explicit reference, and it is hedged with a condition:

> When the penalty of our sin was paid in full by Jesus Christ on the cross, God's wrath was expressed against Him — the One who took our place. God was therefore satisfied in the epochal sacrifice . . . allowing all who would turn, in faith, to the Son of God to be totally, once-for-all, forgiven. (I.S., 57)

Here we see the wrath of God "expressed" against Jesus on the cross, but forgiveness hinges on the turning of the repentant heart. Thus we are partially forgiven because of our decision of faith, not entirely because of Christ's sacrifice. Here the gospel comes dangerously close to being just another "how-to" in the believer's arsenal of techniques to use to tackle his personal inadequacies.

This view of the gospel as man's response to his predicament seems to be reinforced in Swindoll's evaluation of the Lutheran Reformation. In protesting the apathy of our age, he calls for a new Reformation centering around creative communication of scriptural principles to help people respond to the complex issues of our time. In Luther's day, Swindoll contends, the goal centered around "the need for clarification to dispel ignorance" (S.G., 268). Luther's discovery of the gospel is considered information on how to be saved, not the saving work which Christ completed for us by his suffering and death. Rather than calling for the trust of the heart, such information needs to be accepted by the mind and the will.

If you look carefully at the few articulations of the gospel Swindoll presents in these three books, it is clear that they are framed in the context of sanctification, not justification.[3] In these instances the gospel is God's prescription for man's illness. Rather than rescuing us from death and reconciling us unto himself, God was in Christ actually freeing us to reach our full potential, in Swindoll's view. Our hopelessness in our sin, he contends, was that "we were victims of all those impulses and defenses within us" (I.S., 89). When Christ cried out "It is finished" from the cross, he was referring to the power of sin, not its guilt. Now, "no longer does sin reign as victor" (I.S., ibid.).

In these three books it is difficult to find the Jesus of the gospels, who came to "seek and to save what was lost" (Luke 19:10). The Jesus presented here is essentially a lawgiver who provides timeless truths around which people are urged to pattern their lives. The Sermon on the Mount, for example, is characterized as " . . . the most comprehensive delineation in all the New Testament of the Christian counterculture . . . " (I.S., 98). This is no God made flesh proclaiming his radical rescue of his people; this is a new Moses laying down his stringent requirements for discipleship.

The Jesus we meet in the gospels is much more than that. He announces the intervention of God in the world. ("The kingdom of heaven is near," Matthew 4:17.) He is himself God, who speaks by divine authority. ("You have heard it said . . . but I say unto you," Matthew 5:21-48.) He has come not to lay down new laws, but to announce the forgiveness of sins. ("Blessed are the poor in spirit, for theirs is the kingdom of heaven," Matthew 5:3.)

Law

Swindoll views the law of God primarily as a standard of conduct for the Christian. Here the human predicament is our loss of purpose and direction, not our spiritual death. Here the core problem is our apathy, not the judgment of God. In one of the few references to God's judgment in these three books, Swindoll refers to his chastisement in this life, not his eternal condemnation. Quoting the American Puritan fathers, Swindoll asserts that if we don't conquer our pet sins, we must spend our lives "under the smarting rod of God" (S.G., 250).

Once again man occupies the central spotlight. Scriptural truth is equated with information to be grasped by the mind and put into action by the human will. Just as the gospel presented in these books is primarily information about historic events, so the law is also presented as information: principles of divine truth to guide the human will in making decisions. And the law can change things, contends Swindoll: " . . . when truth makes an impact on the will, lives begin to change" (D.G., 164).

Scripture portrays the law in a different light. The law contains no promise; it has no power to produce change in the lives of believers. Rather, "All who rely on observing the law are under a curse, for it is written: 'Cursed is everyone who does not continue to do everything written in the Book of the Law' " (Galatians 3:10).

This is why the Lutheran Confessions are unequivocal in their denial of any power of the law to effect change in the human life:

> We cannot even love an angry God; the law always
> accuses us and thus always shows us an angry God.
> Therefore we must first take hold of the promise by
> faith, that for Christ's sake the Father is reconciled
> and forgiving. Later we begin to keep the law. Far
> away from human reason, far away from Moses, we
> must turn our eyes to Christ, and believe that he was
> given for us to be justified on his account. In the flesh
> we never satisfy the law. Thus we are not accounted
> righteous because of the law but because of Christ,
> whose merits are conferred on us if we believe in him.
> (Apology IV, 295-296)

The above approach to God's law is entirely different from the one advocated by Swindoll. In his view, the law is merely a friend to the Christian, a guide through the many complexities of modern life. In reading the Bible, we are urged to apply its "insights and guidelines" (S.G., 23). The reader gets the definite impression that the central purpose of the Bible is not to bring us to the cross but to provide us with a set of principles to guide our lives.

The Bible Swindoll presents to his readers in these three books is not the dramatic revelation of God's own Son, crucified and risen for the redemption of the world, but rather a loosely connected string of incidents from ancient history through which God shows his children in every age how to live. In the lives of his ancient people, God was really demonstrating to his modern people the kinds of things they must copy or avoid in order to have a life that is fulfilling to them as well as pleasing to him. The Bible, Swindoll reminds his readers, " . . . is full of verses and principles that promise you His commitment" (D.G., 39).

The Bible's own testimony leads in a different direction:

> For everything that was written in the past was written to teach us, so that through endurance and the encouragement of the Scriptures we might have hope. (Romans 15:4)
> ... these are written that you may believe that Jesus is the Christ, the Son of God, and that by believing you may have life in his name. (John 20:31)

Swindoll is absolutely right in his diagnosis of the problem modern Christians find themselves in; his prescription, however, only treats the symptoms. By directing people to the law in order to overcome their lack of spiritual vitality and in order to provide an outer structure for their lives, he only applies a band-aid to the problem. We need stronger medicine: the resuscitating power of Jesus Christ, who grants life and renewal in the word of his gospel.

Success

If the presentation of law and gospel in these books leaves something to be desired, I will hasten to add that Swindoll avoids many of the other noticeable pitfalls of the Evangelical movement. His critique of the "theology of success," for example, shows he is not interested in a perfectionist brand of Christianity. No matter how godly they become, he reminds us, Christians "... are every bit as human and subject to the perils of life as any other person on earth" (I.S., 142).

The Christian portrayed in the books under study is no plastic saint. He is not one who expects an easy life, free of affliction or pain. He does not go through life with a veneer of artificial euphoria covering the hurts within him.

> Surrounded by numerous types to whom everything is "fantastic," "super," and "incredible," let's work hard at being real. This means we are free to question, to admit failure or weakness, to confess wrong, to declare the truth. When a person is authentic, he or she does not have to win or always be in the top ten or make a big impression or look super-duper pious. (S.G., 22)

This kind of honesty is refreshing when compared with the cotton candy fluff passed off as Christianity in many circles today. Jesus told his followers, "In this world you will have trouble" (John 16:33). Far too many teachers these days imply that the Christian will lead a happy, carefree life. But, the Christian hope is not to be found in a trouble-free world. It is always founded upon the promise of Christ: " . . . but take heart! I have overcome the world" (John 16:33).

Swindoll avoids the pitfall of a superficial theology of success and paints a realistic picture of the Christian life as a constant struggle with sin and temptation. One can only applaud such realism. The solutions offered for that struggle, however, often center merely on the encouragement of fellow Christians rather than on the forgiveness of sins and the strength offered by the Holy Spirit through his Word and sacrament. Here a friendly criticism must be raised: it is Jesus who has overcome the world, not the believing community. As the body of Christ proceeds to minister to the hurts of its members, it has nothing better to offer than the love and strength supplied by its Head, Jesus Christ.

Freedom of the will

If Swindoll has charted his own course in his critique of "success theology," he is still quite mainstream with contemporary revivalistic Evangelicalism in his view of the potential of the human will to achieve and maintain a relationship with God.

Over and over again these books stress that man will need to take the first step if he is to experience God's salvation. Conversion is termed "choosing to let Christ come into your life" (D.G., 166), "turning your life over to Christ" (ibid.), "an experience I had" (S.G., 230),and a willingness to turn in faith (I.S., 57).

The Scriptures make it clear that the invitation to faith cannot be accepted by man's will. The very text which serves as the *sedes doctrinae* ("seat of doctrine") for much of modern Evangelicalism demonstrates that no one can enter the kingdom of God unless he is spiritually reborn: whoever is born to sinful parents is a sinner himself, Jesus informs Nicodemus (John 3:6). To come into a relationship with God implies being born all over again by the power of God's Holy Spirit.[4]

"No one can come to me," Jesus informed the Galilean crowd (John 6:44), "unless the Father who sent me draws him." Jesus packed a vivid picture into that little sentence. He chose the word which many in his audience used every day to describe "drawing" a boat up on shore. Boats out of water are notoriously clumsy and decidedly uncooperative, as any fisherman knows. "*You* don't come to me," Jesus was in effect saying, "The *Father* has to drag you to me."

The reason human beings are naturally unresponsive to God is found in Ephesians 2:1: " ... you were dead in your transgressions and sins, in which you used to live." A dead person can't choose anything. The experience which brings us to life is not "choosing Jesus" or "turning our heart over to him" in faith. We don't need a choice; we need a resurrection!

The apostle makes it clear that there is nothing whatsoever within the Christian qualifying him to come on his own power. On the contrary, " . . . we were by nature objects of wrath. But because of his great love for us, God, who is rich in mercy, made us alive with Christ even when we were dead in transgressions . . . " (Ephesians 2:4,5).

Reflecting the Scriptures, the Lutheran Confessions are adamant in denying even the slightest credit to the will of man in his own conversion:

> . . . we believe that after the Fall and prior to his conversion not a spark of spiritual powers has remained or exists in man by which he could make himself ready for the grace of God or to accept the proffered grace, nor that he has any capacity for grace by and for himself or can apply himself to it or prepare himself for it, or help, do, effect, or cooperate toward his conversion by his own powers, either altogether or half-way or in the tiniest or smallest degree, . . . but is a slave of sin (John 8:34), the captive of the devil who drives him (Eph. 2:2; II Tim. 2:26). [F.C.S.D., 118]

Besides claiming an active role for man in his own conversion, Swindoll places the primary emphasis in maintaining the life of faith on the human will. The difference between being a mere Christian and an active disciple, he maintains, is the decision "to let Christ invade every room of your life . . . " (D.G., 26).

The ongoing life of Christian growth and service is presented primarily as making the right moral choices according to the principles revealed in God's Word. This is a very mental activity as it is portrayed by Swindoll. "It is never too late to start doing what is right" (S.G., 203). "It all begins in the mind," he contends. "Let me repeat it one more time. Thinking right always precedes acting right" (I.S., 94).

The careful reader can detect a tension between Swindoll's optimistic view of the power of the human will described above and his realism in portraying the predicament of sin. The natural human mind-set constitutes a wall to the Spirit of God, he writes (I.S., 87). Our natural minds not only resist the principles of the Scriptures, " . . . they ask, 'Who needs that?' or 'I've gotten along pretty good up 'til now' " (I.S., 89).

Which role is played by the human will in the growth of Christian life and service — the biggest obstacle or the greatest force? St. Paul opts for the former: "I know that nothing good lives in me, that is, in my sinful nature. For I have the desire to do what is good, but I cannot carry it out" (Romans 7:18). Consistently, the Scriptures then also deny that the unaided human will can make the right choices even after conversion: "Those who are led by the Spirit are sons of God" (Romans 8:14).

Swindoll's strong emphasis on the power of the human will may be attractive to our "have it your way" age. However, it does not appear to be a faithful reflection of the Scriptural emphasis on the power of God's Holy Spirit as the sole agent in conversion and the incapacity of the renewed will to choose to do good on its own.

Reformed Concepts

Given the extensive influence of Reformed theology in American protestantism, it's not surprising to find that Chuck Swindoll frequently speaks with a distinctly Reformed accent.

For example, Swindoll denies baptismal regeneration. For him, baptism is the "public acknowledgment of. . .faith" (S.G., 234). He argues that in Acts 8 Philip the evangelist is providing a pattern to be followed by Christians of every age. "With decisive discernment," he writes, "Philip explained that faith in Jesus precedes [italics his] baptism" (Ibid.)

It must be asked how such a view can be reconciled with Titus 3:5 where baptism is termed a "washing of regeneration and renewal in the Holy Spirit," and 1 Peter 3:21 where it is asserted that "baptism now saves you." In view of these scriptures, would it not be fairer to regard the order of confession, then baptism as pastoral practice in the case of an adult candidate and leave the door open to a higher view of the power of baptism as a channel for God's offer of grace and faith?[5]

Another strong thread of Reformed theological influence woven skillfully throughout these three books of Swindoll is the theme of the covenant. The suggestion is made that God is somehow bound to respond to people who act in accordance with the principles of his will. "God honors a spirit of unity among His people," Swindoll asserts (D.G., 83). The implication is that God's agreement with Israel is still in effect. As latter-day Hebrews, modern Christians who obey the terms of Israel's contract with the Lord will receive his blessings.

For example, when a Christian couple "makes Christ a vital part of their life . . . that's when 'the Lord builds the house' " (S.G., 257f). Here we must ask if this uncritical adoption of the Old Testament covenant into a New Testament setting is really faithful to the Scriptures. What is actually the motivation of Christians who set out to live by the immense variety of principles listed in these books? Are they looking for something from God?

What about the devout husband and wife who strive to please God, implementing Scriptural guidelines in their marriage, and yet experience hardship and sorrow? Are they to assume that God has backed out of his agreement?

A more realistic approach is one of humility before the internal deliberations of God, the kind of attitude advocated by the Apostle Paul:

> Oh, the depth of the riches of the wisdom and knowledge of God! How unsearchable his judgments, and his paths beyond tracing out! Who has known the mind of the Lord? Or who has been his counselor? (Romans 11:33,34)

God's action does not hinge on ours. He cannot be manipulated into action in response to human obedience to his will. God's will is indeed sovereign. All things actually do work together for good in the life of the Christian, even though now our perception of God's good intention may be "through a glass darkly."[6] Some things cannot be understood this side of eternity. Still, we can say with Job, "Though he slay me, yet will I praise him." Our motivation is not in the future, but in the past. Our service to him is not based on expectation of reward in this life, but on the experience of God's love in Christ.

97

We do not know the internal workings of the will of God for our life. But we do know what he has revealed to us in his Son: that in him there is life eternal beginning here and now for all who trust in him. We may not be able to explain why everything seems to be going against us at times, but we do know one glorious fact: "If God is for us, who can be against us? He who did not spare his own Son, but gave him up for us all — how will he not also, along with him, graciously give us all things?" (Romans 8:31,32)

Finally, there seems to be some confusion in the three books before us as to the function of the sovereignty of God.

On the one hand, the sovereignty of God is a comfort to the Christian. During a time of immense personal and political turmoil, God gave Isaiah a vision of his sovereignty to stabilize him: "Isaiah saw no confused or anxious deity, but One who sat in sovereign, calm control with full perspective and in absolute authority" (S.G., 185). Modern day Christians who are up against affliction are reminded of the absolute sovereignty of the will of God as a source of comfort in their distress. They are asked to remember that "nothing touches me that has not passed through the hands of my heavenly Father. Nothing.... Everything I endure is designed to prepare me for serving others more effectively. Everything" (I.S., 189).

Yet at the same time the awesome holiness of the sovereign God caused Isaiah to despair on account of his sin.

> Isaiah is frightened, beaten, and broken. Not only does he see the Lord sovereign, high and exalted, not only does he witness the antiphonal choir of angels

swarming the heavenly throne, he also hears that God is infinitely holy. And in contrast to his own sinfulness and depravity, he feels doomed ... beaten. (S.G., 186)

Here we see that the sovereignty of God is by no means comforting to someone who is aware of his sin.

If there is confusion about the effect of the sovereignty of God on the Christian, God's remedy for Isaiah's sin is even more confusing as presented by Swindoll. The purging of Isaiah's lips with the red-hot coal from the temple's altar ends up sounding more like law than gospel. When the angel announces the removal of Isaiah's guilt and atonement for his sin ("your guilt is taken away and your sin atoned for"), we hear more command than promise: "What affirmation! Where sin abounded, grace *super* abounded. The one thing Isaiah had been hiding behind, ashamed to admit but unable to conquer, God dealt with" (S.G., 188).

Here we must ask whether the gospel has not been turned into a new law. The forgiveness announced by the angel is not presented as God's gracious word of acquittal to a man terrified by his sin, but the removal of Isaiah's excuse for inaction in carrying out God's command.

No one should be surprised to find Reformed theological themes in sermons preached by a Reformed pastor. The critique offered here is not simply a case of Lutheran "flag waving." We don't need a "my-dad-is-bigger-than-your-dad" pitting of Luther against Calvin. I have tried to be as objective as I can. The real issue is not what Luther said, but what God says. That's why I set out to compare these books with scriptural teaching and then to consider their own inner integrity. It would appear that there are serious problems in various points of doctrine on both counts.

It is not enough to point out problems. If this is a genuinely friendly critique I should be prepared to offer something constructive in place of the problem areas. The last chapter of this book contains some alternative approaches on these issues, approaches which were hinted at already in the occasional references I made to the Lutheran Confessions.

Before offering these alternatives, one more step is necessary. In order to evaluate fairly Swindoll's work, his stated purpose must be considered. His books were written to meet clearly defined problems he sees modern Christians dealing with every day.

Needs and goals addressed by Swindoll

One of the most revealing ways of discovering the thrust of the three books under discusssion is to look at the publisher's publicity on their jacket covers:

> [Swindoll] offers solid footholds and firm grips on the essentials of life in this straightforward book. . . . By asserting timeless and timely principles from Scripture and committed life, the author strengthens timid wills, imparts courage, and rekindles desire for the well-aimed life. . . . Get ready to exchange your halfhearted attitudes for new spiritual vigor as Charles Swindoll shows you how to strengthen your grip on what is really significant in life. (*Strengthening Your Grip*)

> Living an unselfish life is an art you can learn. This book will introduce you to *authentic servanthood* . . . Charles Swindoll offers accurate, clear, and practical help from the Scriptures on how to develop a servant's heart. (*Improving Your Serve*)

> In a society where isolation and loneliness are epidemic . . . where our most intimate comment is a glib "Have a nice day" . . . Charles R. Swindoll offers a

> refreshing and essential alternative: . . . he uses
> Scripture and down-to-earth personal illustrations to
> show how we can begin to enjoy authentic fellowship
> with one another when we dare to put down our
> masks and pretenses and reach out to one another.
> (*Dropping Your Guard*)

As we turn to the content of these books, we discover it is impossible to read them without encountering Swindoll's keen interest in the frustrations, fears, and obstacles confronting today's Christian. He addresses himself to concerns running the full range of human experience.

Loneliness

In our fast-paced world, Americans are finding themselves increasingly isolated from one another. Caught up in the pressures of their individual lives, they have little time to devote to meaningful interaction with others.

> Our world has become a large, impersonal, busy institution. We are alienated from each other. Although crowded, we are lonely. Distant. Pushed together but uninvolved. No longer do most neighbors visit across the backyard fence. The well-manicured front lawn is the modern moat that keeps barbarians at bay. Hoarding and flaunting have replaced sharing and caring. (I.S., 17)

Coupled with personal factors leading to loneliness is the highly mobile nature of our society. The average American moves fourteen times in his lifetime (D.G., 20). No wonder, then, that our worlds are lonely worlds. Swindoll suggests that a first step toward getting rid of that loneliness is to come out from behind the masks we all hide behind (D.G., 206).

The prescription for loneliness he recommends is involvement — with God, with family members, other Christians and with non-Christians (S.G., 31).

Interaction with others

Human beings were not designed to live lives of isolation. Swindoll's single objective in writing *Dropping Your Guard* is: "I would like to convince you of the value of open relationships" (D.G., 10). In order to be open toward others, we are going to have to overcome our modern tendency toward an "independent, self-sufficient, survival-of-the-fittest mentality" (I.S., 210). In addition, we must go against the tide of our age. The new slogan of the 1980s has become: "Who really cares?" (S.G, 13)

> The muscular patriot who once rolled up his sleeves and dared any enemy to step foot on our shores [is] now listening to the clicks of a computer, preoccupied in his silent, isolated world of code language all day and the glare of color television half the night. The tide of apathy has risen, and we are seeing the sand castles that once housed our hopes washed out to sea. (Ibid.)

The best way to begin meaningful interaction with others, Swindoll suggests, is to be involved with a particular person or group of Christians in a relationship which is mutually accountable and genuinely in touch with one another's needs (D.G., 180). Christian leaders must learn how to avoid pushing people around and begin to lead by example more than by directives. "[Christians] respond more like sheep than steers" (D.G., 161).

We need to learn the basic Scriptural principles of how to love others (D.G., 122). Men in particular seem to have great difficulty in learning how to have meaningful friendships with other men (D.G., 116). There is nothing that builds positive relationships with people more effectively than giving them meaningful encouragement (D.G., 84). Personal friction arising from conflicts with others is the barrier to meaningful interaction with others (D.G., 102). Christian forgiveness is the key to erasing the bitterness that lingers because of conflict (I.S., 66ff), and the Christian must learn to make the first move toward reconciliation with someone he or she has offended (I.S., 60).

Self

In his book focusing on various issues confronting Christians in the eighties, Swindoll devotes several chapters to topics of a primarily personal nature. In his chapter on encouragement, he shows how to overcome personal defeat by effective affirmation (S.G., 42ff). There is no greater way to develop a good reputation than to practice Christian integrity (S.G., 88ff). Christians must learn to gain a biblical perspective on aging (S.G., 128ff). In order to avoid burnout because of the great demands on our emotions and energies, Christians should learn the biblical principles governing leisure (S.G., 160ff).

If we want to attain a healthy self-image, Swindoll suggests that we learn to practice authentic humility (I.S., 41). Lasting happiness is to be found in putting the beatitudes of Jesus into practice (I.S., 99). Even if we feel used and unappreciated in our life of servanthood, we must remember, "Our God who rewards in secret will never overlook your commitment" (I.S., 148).

In order to fulfill their potential as salt of the earth and light for the world, Christians must learn to be different from the world around them, responsible in their actions, and aware of the influence they have in the world (I.S., 136f).

Values

Contemporary society suffers from a general deterioration of moral fiber. Swindoll stresses the reassertion of divinely revealed moral principles as a means of recovering a God-pleasing system of values. As the American family is under attack, scriptural principles governing parents and spouses should be recovered (S.G., 252ff). In our age of sexual promiscuity, Christians should genuinely be striving for moral purity (S.G., 55ff).

In general, our age of moral decay calls for the re-establishment of sound Scriptural foundations to provide guidance for Christians living in a world which seems to have lost its way.

> We need biblical fixed points to hang on to — firm, solid handles that will help us steer our lives in a meaningful manner. What we really want is something to grab — believable, reliable truth that makes sense for today's generation, essential principles for our aimless world. (S.G., 14)

Affliction

The Christian must contend with opposition in his life from the devil, the world, and his own sinful nature. Drawing from scriptural principles, Swindoll prescribes a way to handle a number of these afflictions.

In our age of materialism, it is necessary to have a firm grip on how to avoid the pitfalls surrounding money (S.G., 71ff). As we deal with more and more violence and depravity in society, we should rediscover what Jesus meant by calling his followers salt and light in the world (I.S., 131). Coping with the strains of pressure, loneliness, stress, and fatigue in our modern pace of life, Christians should realize the benefits of sharing those burdens in genuine openness to others (S.G., 46).

Above all, while undergoing various afflictions, it is necessary for the Christian to have a proper attitude. This involves trust in the will of the heavenly Father (I.S., 189f) and a positive outlook of humility and joy (S.G., 205ff).

Spiritual growth

In order to continue to grow in personal faith, the Christian must recognize and deal with the barriers to spiritual maturity (D.G., 38). He should cultivate the practice of prayer (S.G., 146ff). He must consciously seek to build a life of personal piety, putting into practice the scriptural themes of godliness (S.G., 194ff).

Swindoll suggests the Christian seriously count the cost of being a follower of Christ (I.S., 48) and rediscover the positive principles of discipleship (S.G., 108ff). Rather than disobeying God (D.G., 104), the Christian should consciously strive to overcome his own mental barriers to divine truth (I.S., 87). The key to developing a God-pleasing life is one's own will; Swindoll contends:

> Before the ink on these pages can be permanently transferred to a change, first in your thinking and then in your living, there must be a willing spirit that says, "Lord, show me ... teach me ... help me ... to serve and to give." If you will let that be your attitude, the process involved in your becoming more like Christ Himself will be much smoother, much faster, and much less painful. (I.S., 13)

Two other important factors in spiritual growth are the development of open relationships with fellow Christians (D.G., 184) and genuine servanthood, which is a real avenue to experiencing God's power in our life in Swindoll's opinion (I.S., 91). The motivation for the Christian's life as a servant is simply and purely obedience to Jesus (I.S., 161ff).

Church life

In these three books, Swindoll also touches on the structure of contemporary church life. Rather than being sanitized, cold and artificial institutions, churches should be genuine places of refuge for people fleeing the hurts and aches of life (D.G., 128). The key ingredient in keeping a church alive is the cultivation of open relationships among its members (D.G., 194). We need to recognize that the people who visit our churches are "greatly in need of affirmation, authentic love, compassion, big doses of esteem, hope, and forgiveness . . . " (D.G., 153).

Church leaders ought not expect those who are coping with burnout and fatigue to be active in their congregations at all times, Swindoll reminds us (D.G., 100). Nor should leaders be discouraged by the obstacles Satan places in the path of growing churches (D.G., 200).

Evaluation

Swindoll has a great interest in people living under the stresses and strains of life. The advertisement for one of his more recent books demonstrates its thrust:

> Are you tired of being caught up in the struggles of modern living? Tired of job, money and social pres-

sures that keep you on the ragged edge? If so, you'll be
encouraged and renewed by this no-nonsense book
from one of today's most beloved Christian spokesmen! Charles Swindoll explores the pressures of
modern living and offers exciting positive guidelines
to help you find the peace and energy you need to not
just survive, but *thrive*![7]

The words above serve to support my thesis: the
central thrust of popular Evangelical teaching is toward sanctification, and it is on this front that
Evangelicalism presents its clearest challenge to
Lutheran theology.

Contemporary Christians certainly are living on
the "ragged edge" of life. Pressures inside and outside are taking their toll on people who are asking
some very real questions: How can I cope with the
hassles of life? How can I face each day with hope in
the face of what seems to be impending disaster on
the global scene and total chaos in my personal life?
What does it mean to be a Christian spouse, parent,
employee or employer in the latter part of the twentieth century? Where can I meet God in the midst of
the maze of my complex life? How can I sense his
power and direction — Where in the world is God?

No Christian could deny the validity of questions
like these. If you want to be a serious disciple of Jesus
Christ today, you simply have to tackle these issues.
Therefore any theological system must be prepared
to respond to the dilemma Swindoll addresses, the
dilemma of living as a Christian in an antagonistic
culture.

Looking at it this way, it is easier to give an honest
evaluation of Swindoll's work. There is no doubt that
the message of these three books is presented effec-

tively and winsomely. Nor is there any doubt that the needs and goals he suggests for contemporary Christians are absolutely crucial. With few exceptions, there is little to question in his conclusions. We still must ask, however, if the way he arrives at those conclusions is faithful to the gospel.

We have already seen[8] how little gospel is contained in these books. What gospel we do find is used primarily as another form of command, not motivation for the sanctified life. The books are essentially lists of "how-tos" for the Christian life, what to do and not to do in order to make sense out of the complex world we live in. The issues of modern life are never examined in light of the good news, but only in light of the proscriptions and prescriptions of the law of God.

If the modern Christian's dilemma stems from living in an antagonistic culture, then we can profitably learn from the New Testament. Here the apostles were delineating a "life style" for Christians who lived in a world completely at odds with everything they stood for. As we look to the letters of the New Testament, we find many statements describing what the new life in Christ means for everyday stresses and strains. Never, however, do these statements of law stand on their own. Always they are undergirded by the life-giving and empowering gospel of Jesus Christ.

Life for the apostles is not viewed as a complex chain of obstacles to overcome by practicing a long list of commands God has prescribed for every contingency. The hostility we encounter in this world can't be chalked up to the quirks of the human mind. Rather, the New Testament recognizes one sinister enemy behind all of the sins and turmoils of life, both internal and external. He is Satan, the father of lies (John 8:44), the ruler of darkness (Ephesians 6:12), the one who accuses God's people in his presence day and night (Revelation 12:10). God's perfect creation has been invaded by this evil adversary and he can now be called the prince of this world (John 14:30).

Entering this enemy-occupied world, Jesus Christ has assumed human flesh to deal with Satan on his own turf (Galatians 4:5). In the body of his flesh he has made satisfaction for the sins of the whole world and defeated the devil by his death and resurrection (Colossians 2:14,15). To all who believe in him he promises everlasting life (John 11:26). Those who trust in him are credited with his very holiness (2 Corinthians 5:21). Drawing on this faith relationship, there is light and life in this world of darkness and death (John 1:4).

No wonder, then, that the apostles were always framing their description of the new life in Christ in the context of Christ's death and resurrection on their behalf. In everything they had to tell the faithful about living the Christian life, they had one focus and one focus only: "I resolved to know nothing while I was with you except Jesus Christ and him crucified" (1 Corinthians 2:2). *The entire life of Christian service should be viewed as Christ's action being carried out in the life of the believer*: "I have been crucified with Christ and I no longer live, but Christ lives in me. The life I live in the body, I live by faith in the Son of God, who loved me and gave himself for me" (Galatians 2:20).

The difference is striking. Most of the Evangelical world puts the spotlight on the Christian's action; the New Testament focuses on Christ's action.

But we need to do more than sit on the sidelines and criticize. Anybody can be an armchair quarterback; after the game is over you know exactly which plays should have been called. It's high time Lutherans got out into the game of sanctification. Chuck Swindoll has put his finger on the crying needs of Christians today. What, if anything, can we do to tackle those needs?

5

CHRIST IN ACTION: A LUTHERAN VIEW OF SANCTIFICATION, MORE THAN A LIFE STYLE

> It is sure that since justification is the mother of sanctification the chief stress will always be laid on the word of forgiveness. But since the daughter "sanctification" though she cannot beget the mother "forgiveness" can destroy her, the significance of sanctification must be presented with all emphasis in evangelical preaching.[1]

> Our churches also teach that this faith is bound to bring forth good fruits and that it is necessary to do the good works commanded by God. We must do so because it is God's will and not because we rely on such works to merit justification before God, for forgiveness of sins and justification are apprehended by faith, as Christ himself also testifies, "When you have done all these things say, 'We are unworthy servants' " (Luke 17:10). (The Augsburg Confession, ArticleVI., "The New Obedience")

How are Christians to find their way through the maze of life at the end of the twentieth century? Are there any alternatives other than the route marked out by Evangelicalism? Is there another road to travel besides the one fenced in by subjectivism and littered with the wreckage of failed attempts to keep the law?

From the traveler's perspective, it appears not. The only real option for meaningful Christian commitment seems to be the kind of "life style" Christianity I have described. In the public eye Evangelicals occupy the focus of attention. They have the largest share of the airwaves, and they have an almost exclusive monopoly on the religious book industry.

American Christians, including some who bear the name "Lutheran," have largely come to see Lutheranism as a one-way street; always reciting its justification formula but unable to put it into practice. This book is dedicated to re-opening that street for two-way traffic. I would like to help clear away the accumulated clutter and remove the detour signs that have led many Lutherans to abandon their sacramental heritage and turn down the road of experiential religion and revivalism.

Do Lutherans have anything at all to offer people struggling to hang on to their faith and cope with the temptations of our age, or will we abandon the field to the New Evangelicals? People today want more than formulas; they want a faith which is a living reality. Christians want help for the daily life of sanctification, and they are looking for more than just pious generalities. Are we willing to take the initiative?

Conservative Lutherans have shown great agility when it comes to defending their doctrinal system against perceived threats. Evangelicals are presenting a clear challenge on the doctrine of sanctification. I'm suggesting, however, that rather than spring into the usual defensive posture, what we really ought to do is to become leaders in the area of sanctification. We need to take the initiative — not just showing the truth of Lutheran teaching, but also its great practicality, to say nothing of its evangelical heart! Out of love for our Lord and his church, it's high time we put our rich heritage into action.

The foundation of sanctification

Christ in me or for me?

We have already seen how Evangelicalism has inherited from Calvin a tendency to place sanctification over justification as the central thrust and end goal of the Christian gospel. Christ's action *in me* is held to be of more importance than Christ's action *for me.*

Not everyone within the Evangelical camp is convinced of the validity of this approach to the faith. In his *Essentials of Evangelical Thought*, Donald Bloesch advances an alternative. Quoting John T. Mueller's *Christian Dogmatics*, he endorses the Lutheran position:

> Besides being the work of God *for us* in Jesus Christ, grace is also the work of God *in us* through the gift of the Holy Spirit. Yet our trust should not be in our own inner renewal, in the presence of grace in our hearts, but only in Christ's perfect work of redemption, the objective reconciliation effected by him.[2]

The proper balance

This is the scriptural relationship between justification and sanctification; it avoids two equally dangerous extremes. Whenever guilty consciences are directed to the inner life for certainty of salvation, faith is immediately in jeopardy, because the Spirit's work inside the Christian is always hampered by the sinful nature. Our sinful nature, St. Paul wrote, has not a single inclination toward good: "I know that nothing good lives in me, that is, in my flesh" (Romans 7:18).

On the other hand, when faith is held to have no connection with life and the sanctifying power of the Spirit is denied, God's gift of grace is robbed of its power. Thus James can conclude: "As the body without the spirit is dead, so faith without deeds is dead" (James 2:26).

The pietistic pitfall

The danger of seeking security in the inner life has been uppermost in Lutheran thinking ever since the age of Pietism, for Pietists elevated the importance of the sanctified life to central place.

The rampant subjectivism and emotionalism of the Pietists was inimical to the heart of the gospel. They exchanged the "alien righteousness" of Christ for the inherent righteousness of the believer as the basis of hope for everlasting life. The Christ *for me* was rejected as a relic of dead orthodoxy in favor of the dynamic work of the Christ *in me*. The invisible verdict of justification *coram Deo* ("before God"), whereby God declares us not guilty for the sake of Christ, was set aside in favor of the visible work of sanctification in the life of the Christian.

Lindberg has commented on the fundamental conflict between Pietism and Luther's thought:

For Pietism the verification of faith lies in its ethical achievement, in its "fruits." The reborn, the new person, refers to a quality of being, a higher nature, which takes effect and becomes visible. Luther on the contrary focuses on the battle between the old and new man, the conflict expressed in his phrase "*simul justus et peccator*" [translation: "at the same time saint and sinner"]. For both Luther and Pietism, rebirth was a process, but while the Pietists directed their attention toward the goal and affirmed the process for its sake, Luther did not. For Luther, victory remains the judgment of God. . . .[3]

Recovering a lost heritage

Having been burned by the abuses of Pietism, Lutheranism has shown an understandable reluctance to deal with the scriptural themes of the new life in Christ. Perhaps the time has come, however, to recapture some of the rich teachings of the Lutheran heritage on the subject. The challenge on the Evangelical front is being mounted on this very issue, and it will not go away by ignoring it.

With few exceptions, the history of Lutheran teaching and church life has shown a consistent distrust of the subjective, or personal, aspect of faith.

Yet also in its heritage the Lutheran church has consistently acknowledged the feelings of the renewed heart. Luther's well-known narrative of his discovery of the gospel is a case in point. After he discovered that the scriptural term "righteousness of God" is a passive righteousness credited to the sinner through faith for the sake of Christ, he wrote: " . . . I felt that I was altogether born again and had entered paradise itself through open gates."[4]

115

Despite his insistence that faith must always be based on the external Word, Luther also spoke of the reality and necessity of the inner life. In fact, I would argue that Luther's adamant stand on the Word alone was in support of, not in opposition to, the new life. Paradoxically, for him it remained unshakably true that the more external the foundation of salvation, the more internal were its results. To the very degree that the objective promises of God in Christ were stressed, to that degree the subjective fruits of the gospel increased in the Christian life. Thus in his masterful explanation to the Second Article of the Creed Luther could speak about the objective reality of the person and work of Christ ("Who has redeemed me, a lost and condemned creature, purchased and won me from all sins, from death and from the power of the devil . . . ") and at the same time about the subjective reality of what that means for the Christian life (" . . . that I may be his own, and live under him in his kingdom, and serve him in everlasting righteousness, innocence and blessedness").[5]

The Word, not feelings

In responding to the Evangelical challenge, we must clearly point out the inherent instability of a theology based on feeling. Luther found from his own experience that feelings can't be trusted because they always undermine the message of the objective Word:

> If you are not ready to believe that the Word is worth more than all you see or feel, then reason has blinded faith. So the resurrection of the dead is something that must be believed. I do not feel the resurrection of

Christ but the Word affirms it. I feel sin but the Word says that it is forgiven to those who believe. I see that Christians die like other men, but the Word tells me that they shall rise again. So we must not be guided by our own feelings but by the Word.[6]

A new initiative

The contemporary theological pendulum has once again swung too far to the side of subjective feelings. Rather than deny the validity of religious feeling, however, Lutherans can show how these feelings are the natural outcome of a faith based on the objective promises of God. Lutherans must do more than react against the subjective Evangelical challenge; the time has come to go on to the next step. It's time to take the initiative and demonstrate the integrity and faithfulness of Lutheran teaching to the Scriptures as well as its practicality in answering the real questions of our age.

A personal journey

Below I offer some first steps toward that new initiative. They have been steps in my own journey, a journey toward a viable and vital Christian faith and life. I invite Lutheran and Evangelical alike to travel with me.

Please understand as we set out that I'm not charting a new course. Most worth-while journeys are traveled on well-worn paths, and this one is no exception. There is little new terrain to be covered on this trip; many guides have blazed the trail ahead of us. I would just like to clear the path a bit.

Where in the world . . . ?

The steps I suggest lead toward the certainty of salvation. The real challenge of Evangelicalism in the area of sanctification is not so much about personal holiness as it is about epistemology — how we come to know about God. Modern man no longer has a Calvinist world view: he is not primarily concerned with obedience to a sovereign God. Today we have a more basic concern: How and where do I find God in the first place? People are asking *"Where in the world is God?"*

Proof for God's reality?

The real attraction of the Evangelical movement, therefore, is not its doctrine of the renewed life in itself, but rather how that renewed life provides demonstrable proof of the reality of God and his action in the world.[7] Carter Lindberg has described the current American scene very well:

> The credibility of the church rests on the changed lives of its people, thus only the praise-filled experience of God's presence and power is the answer to today's experience of insecurity and uncertainty. The depersonalization of contemporary life in the midst of materialism and secularism disposes persons to search for a personal experience of reality.[8]

Jesus' experience, not ours

There is another alternative. Rather than seeking the reality of God in our own experience, the Bible directs us to find assurance in the historic events of God's intervention in this world in the person and life of his Son. The basis of our knowledge about God and his living, vibrant reality is not in our experience, but in the experience of Jesus on the cross. There he faced the wrath of the Father and made satisfaction for the sins of the whole world. In his triumphant resurrection, there is validation of his entire saving work. In the word of his gospel, we have no mere static facts about events of history, but the actual means by which people of every age may be brought into genuine contact with the saving work of Christ. "It [the gospel] is the power of God for the salvation of everyone who believes" (Romans 1:16).

The power for sanctification

Whoever drinks the water I give him will never thirst. Indeed, the water I give him will become in him a spring of water welling up to eternal life. (John 4:14)

I have been crucified with Christ and I no longer live, but Christ lives in me. The life I live in the body, I live by faith in the Son of God, who loved me and gave himself for me. (Galatians 2:20)

Current Evangelical literature, with its myriad of principles, warm folksy illustrations, and down to earth advice, presents the power for the new life as a combination of man's work and God's work. Sure, God saves me by grace, but then he expects me to perform. With his Spirit he gives me the power I need to get started, but then it's up to me. By following his principles and continuing in close fellowship with him and my fellow believers, I will be inspired to produce the kind of life that is pleasing to him. Spectacular power is available; all I have to do is reach out and grab it!

119

Do-it-yourself Christians

Thus we see that self-assertion once again raises its ugly head. Pride is deeply ingrained in the human nature. No one likes to be told he can't do something; in fact, each of us enjoys taking credit for our accomplishments. So also when it comes to the Christian faith. There is something deep within us that rebels when Scripture reminds us that there is nothing we can do to save ourselves:

> For it is by grace you have been saved, through faith — and this is not from yourselves, it is the gift of God — not by works, so that no one can boast. (Ephesians 2:8,9)

Similarily, we do not like to hear that God himself is the driving power in our life of sanctification:

> For we are God's workmanship, created in Christ Jesus to do good works, which God prepared in advance for us to do. (Ephesians 2:10)

True, Scripture does speak of the activity of the Christian in performing works of love: " ... continue to work out your salvation with fear and trembling. ... " At the same time, however, we are reminded that the power for the sanctified life is not our own: " ... for it is God who works in you to will and to act according to his good purpose" (Philippians 2:12,13).

A package deal

Justification (God's action to save us) and sanctification (our life of service to him) are to be clearly separated temporally and theologically, but not essentially. Like the proverbial horse and cart, they can neither be unhitched nor rehitched. Putting sanctification before justification is an affront to God's grace and a stumbling block to faith. Holding to justification without sanctification leads nowhere, for "faith without works is dead" (James 2:26). No one setting out on a journey in a horse-drawn cart hitches the cart in front of the horse, nor does he shoot the horse. Together they make a unit. Yet clearly the horse has to come first and provide the power if there is to be any forward movement!

> Sanctification describes the same reality as does justification but describes the justified Christian's relationship to the world and society. Justification and sanctification are not two separate realities, but the same reality viewed from the different perspectives of God and man. From the perspective of God the reality of the Christian is totally passive and non-contributory as it receives Christ only. From the perspective of the world, the same reality never ceases in its activity and tirelessly performs all good works.[9]

Jesus only

Thus when speaking about the power for the sanctified life, we dare never stop speaking about Christ. St. Paul put it this way: "For I resolved to know nothing while I was with you except Jesus Christ and him crucified" (1 Corinthians 2:2). The person and work of the crucified Lord is the sum total of our message. He is all in all — "our righteousness, our sanctification, and our redemption" (1 Corinthians 1:30).[10] No wonder, then, that Luther could write, "Having been justified by grace, we then do good works, yes, Christ himself does all in us."[11]

121

Christ in action: the incarnation

... Who for us men and for our salvation came down
from heaven and was incarnate by the Holy Spirit of
the virgin Mary, and was made man....

(The Nicene Creed, ca. 325 A.D.)

Looking for God in a hostile world

If the central religious problem for medieval man
was finding a merciful God, modern man's problem
is finding God at all. Looking around himself in an
increasingly technological and impersonal world, he
sees nothing but despair and confusion. A newspa-
per cartoon pictures one character asking another:
"Do you believe there is a god?" The other replies:
"Well, *somebody's out to get me!*"

Since the empirical evidence seems to go nowhere,
modern Americans are inclined to look inside themselves for indications of the reality of God and his
power. No one, after all, can challenge a person's
own emotions. If I *feel* the presence of God, he must
be real!

In our subjective age, the lure of this approach to
Christian certainty cannot be underestimated. In
the emotional peaks of spiritual experience, today's
American Christian finds convincing proof of the
reality of God. He has found a ladder by which he can
climb into the very presence of God. He has found a
new evidential base for a faith that seems to have no
other foundation in our hostile world: his own feelings.

The Jesus connection

Scripture, however, holds out a different foundation for the spiritual life: Jesus Christ.

122

> In the past God spoke to our forefathers through the
> prophets at many times and in various ways, but in
> these last days he has spoken to us by his Son . . .
> (Hebrews 1:1,2)

The reality of God and the power of his presence are
not to be found in human experience, but in the person and work of Jesus. He is the eternal Word of the
Father, through whom all created beings were called
into existence, and who has taken on human flesh in
order to bring to us the power of the divine life.

"The Word became flesh and lived for a while
among us" (John 1:14). Here is the only legitimate
connection between humanity and its creator. It is a
connection established on God's initiative, not ours.
He has come to us because we could not go to him. If
we want reliable information about God, we should
seek him not in the interior of our own heart, but in
his external Word and promise in Jesus Christ.

God in a manger

The Christmas shepherds provide us with an
interesting case study. They did not experience true
knowledge of God and real contact with him in their
glorious hillside vision of the heavenly armies, but
at the stable where they looked upon the eternal God
lying helpless in the hay. This is where the eternal
meets the temporal and where the spiritual joins the
material. This is where God meets man!

> [True Christian theology always begins] . . . where
> Christ began — in the Virgin's womb, in the manger,
> and at his mother's breasts. For this purpose he came
> down, was born, lived among men, suffered, was
> crucified and died, so that in every possible way he
> might present himself to our sight. He wanted us to
> fix the gaze of our hearts upon himself and thus to

> prevent us from clambering into heaven and specu-
> lating about the Divine Majesty.[12]

To be sure, the infant wrapping cloths and hay of the manger were not places that man would expect to meet God, but this is exactly where God chose to meet man. He clothed himself in lowly human flesh so that he might come into contact with his sinful creatures without annihilating them with his righteous glory.

God on a cross

This incarnation, or taking on of human flesh, is not only the means by which God has made contact with the world, but it is also the means by which he has saved the world from sin. Jesus said:

> I am the living bread that came down from heaven. If a man eats of this bread, he will live forever. This bread is my flesh, which I will give for the life of the world. (John 6:51)

Offering himself in payment for the guilt of the world, the eternal Son of God, who cannot die, took on mortal flesh. He "bore our sins in his body" at the cross (1 Peter 2:24). Thus the Apostle Paul could write, "He has reconciled you by Christ's physical body through death to present you holy in his sight, without blemish and free from accusation" (Colossians 1:22). By his real death and real resurrection, Christ has purchased real forgiveness and real life with the Father for all who believe in him.

The spiritual/material problem

The early church went through a great many controversies trying to understand how Jesus could possibly be both God and man at the same time. In the fifth century Nestorius was accused of teaching of "two Christs," one human and one divine.

Our age, too, has its problems with the relationship between heavenly and earthly things. All too often Christians practice a kind of Nestorian piety which separates the human from the divine. Only spiritual matters are considered worthy of God's consideration. The earthly, material and physical part of human existence is looked down upon and every attempt is made to transform it into a spiritual dimension. People go to a lot of trouble to manufacture a "Christian" environment in which to live and work. Rather than being transformed by the renewal of their own minds, these Christians attempt to transform earth into heaven. It is time to look at the ideal Christian environment being advocated today and ask whether this insulated existence is not in reality a new monastic movement.

But there is a much more serious question. Isn't the inordinate compulsion to buy "Christian" products, to patronize "Christian" businesses, to watch "Christian" television, to read "Christian" publications, and to listen exclusively to "Christian" music actually a denial of the incarnation? Isn't this really a rejection of what God did when he became man, taking on the material of this physical world?

The radical alternative

There is another route. It is the alternative of a Christian piety which finds its source in the God-made-flesh, Jesus Christ. He did not despise the material, but redeemed it. He did not reject the physical, but assumed it. He did not flee from the world, but rescued it.

The New Testament speaks of a Christian life molded by faith in this God-man. Here there is no rigid division between the physical and the spiritual: " . . . I urge you, brothers, in view of God's mercy, to offer your bodies as living sacrifices, holy and pleasing to God — which is your spiritual worship" (Romans 12:1). Rather than building a wall around ourselves, we are asked to take an active role in the real world, "making the most of every opportunity, because the days are evil" (Ephesians 5:16). The most ordinary and routine activity becomes a way of demonstrating our faith in God: "So whether you eat or drink or whatever you do, do it all for the glory of God" (1 Corinthians 10:31). And even the lowliest gesture has a spiritual dimension: " . . . if anyone gives a cup of cold water to one of these little ones because he is my disciple, I tell you the truth, he will certainly not lose his reward" (Matthew 10:42).

This approach to the Christian life is radically different from the one we see in much of the Evangelical world. There is a reason it is radically different. It is built on the most radical thing in the world —the cross of Christ.

Christ in action: the cross

Carrying his own cross, he went out to the Place of the Skull (which in Aramaic is called Golgotha). Here they crucified him. (John 19:17,18)

We preach Christ crucified: a stumbling block to Jews and foolishness to Gentiles, but to those whom God has called, both Jews and Greeks, Christ the power of God and the wisdom of God. [1 Corinthians 1:23,24]

The crucifixion of Jesus Christ stands as the greatest paradox in history. There God hid in lowly weakness to show himself to us, there God humiliated himself to give us glory, and there God died to give us life!

The hidden God

It's no wonder people ask, "Where in the world is God?" The Bible makes it clear that he can't be found by human senses or intellect. To be sure, his "eternal power and divine nature have been clearly seen" in the world around us (Romans 1:20), but all we can detect in this way is his wrath. The fullness of his love is experienced only when he discloses himself to us.

The God of the Bible is a God who is unreachable by human effort and unattainable through human reason. When people come into contact with him, it is because he has revealed himself to them:

> The man without the Spirit does not accept the things that come from the Spirit of God, for they are foolishness to him, and he cannot understand them, because they are spiritually discerned. (1 Corinthians 2:14)

It's not surprising that created beings should be incapable of reaching the Creator under their own power. Since we cannot comprehend him with our minds, we aren't surprised to find that God is hidden to us. The really astounding thing is that God is actually hiding himself from us: "Truly you are a God who hides himself, O God and Savior of Israel" (Isaiah 45:15).

This does not square with the picture of God everyone has in his or her mind. But that's just the problem: the god conjured up in the human imagination is only a projection of our own feelings. The god of human speculation is a false god, he does not exist! Human beings always like to make God over in their own image. But that god is an idol. The real God of heaven and earth is a God who hides himself.

The seeking God

God isn't playing games with us, however. As we look to the Scriptures, we see that God is more interested in seeking than hiding. Right after our first parents sinned, God came searching for them: "Adam, where are you?" (Genesis 3:9) Jesus defended his concern for a social outcast: "The Son of Man came to seek and to save what was lost" (Luke 19:10). There's no doubt about it; our God is a seeking God. He won't allow us to hide from him. His love is too strong for that.

Why, then, should he hide from us? Why doesn't he reveal himself openly and unmistakably and powerfully? That would be the best way to give us comfort and strength in our troubled world, we think. Like Moses, we are not content with God's bare promises. We ask impatiently: "Now show me your glory" (Exodus 33:18).

But God loves us too much to honor our request. Sinful human beings cannot tolerate God's unveiled majesty and glory. If God would come to us in his power, we would be annihilated by his holiness. "No one may see me and live," he told Moses. (Exodus 33:20) And so God hid his glory from Moses in order to preserve his life. He permitted Moses only a glimpse from his hiding place in the cleft of a rock.

Letting God be God

"Where in the world is God?" That's the real issue. People today, not satisfied with what appears to be God's silence, are still asking for some proof of his existence, some evidence of his reality. Eager for some demonstration of his power, they look to their own emotional experiences in order to find God. But he can't be found there.

God has promised to reveal himself only in certain places; and the human heart isn't one of them. "Out of the heart come evil thoughts, murder, adultery, sexual immorality, theft, false testimony, slander," Jesus said (Matthew 15:19).

Remember, our God is a God who *hides* in order to make himself known. And he hides in the strangest places! — In the Word of the gospel proclaimed in human speech and attached to the humble elements of water, bread, and wine. Through these channels he still comes into intimate contact with people, just as he did when he hid in a virgin's womb, a manger, a cross and a tomb. If we are to find God, we have to let God be God. We must seek him where he has promised to be found!

The sign of Jonah

In the sixteenth chapter of Matthew, we have a remarkable sequence of events that helps us understand how God operates through the cross of his Son in direct opposition to every human expectation.

The Pharisees and Sadducees speak for all of us, asking Jesus to prove his identity (v. 1). We all would like to know where in the world God is, and we would like him to make himself perfectly and unmistakably evident. Jesus, however, makes it clear that there will be no miraculous evidence given. The only evidence will be the "sign of Jonah" (v. 4). The strange three-day sea journey of the Old Testament prophet in the fish's stomach was really a picture of the three-day burial of Jesus.

You can't be any more hidden than Jonah was in a fish belly under the water. Jesus makes the extraordinary claim that he would be no less hidden: people would be able to see who he was when his lifeless body would be placed into a tomb for three days. To ask for any more proof than his death is foolhardy and dangerous; it is following the teachings ("yeast") of the Pharisees and Sadducees (v. 5-12).

Church growth

You just can't arrive at the identity of Jesus by reason or intellectual deduction. When Peter made his glowing confession that Jesus was "the Christ, the Son of the living God" (v. 16), Jesus explained that Peter had not arrived at this conviction by human ingenuity. God the Father had revealed it to him.

Whenever people come to faith, it is always on God's initiative. Jesus make its clear that this is the permanent pattern for the growth of his church; he himself will build it as the Father brings people to confess that he is Christ and God (v. 18,19).

The satanic pitfall

Immediately after Peter's confession of faith, Jesus begins to explain what his saving work includes: first torture at the hands of the power structure in Jerusalem, then execution and, only after that, resurrection (v. 21). Peter is horrified. "This shall never happen to you!" he exclaims (v. 22).

What Jesus has to say to Peter at this point stands for all time as a clear condemnation of every effort to find God through human reason and speculation:

"Out of my sight, Satan! . . . you do not have in mind the things of God, but the things of men" (v. 23). The "things of men" always run directly opposite to the "things of God." The things of men focus on glory and power; the things of God center in weakness and the cross. Human eyes are always on the heights; God's eyes are always on the depths.

> God chose the foolish things of the world to shame the wise; God chose the weak things of the world to shame the strong. He chose the lowly things of this world and the despised things — and the things that are not — to nullify the things that are, so that no one may boast before him. (1 Corinthians 1:27,28)

Where in the world is God? We want to know. We all want to know. The yeast of the Pharisees and Sadducees is still with us, prodding us to look for God in the experiences of our mind and heart. But we have to let God be God. We have to let him speak where he has promised to speak to us: from the cross of Jesus, his son!

The word from the cross

If we listen to our hearts alone, we will not hear God. We will only be talking to ourselves. This is deception and leads us astray. Instead, we must look to God on the cross. This is where God is revealed. We hear him speak to us there. And it is a message of hope and joy, even though it cannot be heard apart from faith: "For the message of the cross is foolishness to those who are perishing, but to us who are being saved it is the power of God" (1 Corinthians 1:18). The cross of Jesus Christ is God's drastic solution to a drastic problem.

131

The real problem

Most people think that the human dilemma is that our lives are out of adjustment; we don't meet God's expectations. Salvation then becomes a matter of rearranging our priorities and adjusting our life style to correspond with God's will. In its crassest form this error leads people to think they earn their own salvation. More often in today's Evangelical world the error has a more subtle disguise: armed with forgiveness through Jesus, people are urged to practice the techniques and principles Christ gave to bring their life style back into line.

It's certainly true that sinful lives are out of adjustment. We're all in need of the Spirit's sanctifying power. But that comes only after our real problem is solved. Sins are just the symptom; our real dilemma is death.

God's final solution

God warned Adam and Eve that the knowledge of evil came with a high price tag: " ... when you eat of it [the tree of the knowledge of good and evil] you will surely die" (Genesis 2:17). Our first parents wanted to be like God and were willing to pay the price. And we are still paying the price: "The wages of sin is death ... " (Romans 6:23). " ... in Adam all die" (1 Corinthians 15:22). " . . . you were dead in your transgressions and sins" (Ephesians 2:1).

The real problem we all face is death. Physical death, to be sure. But ultimately and most horribly, spiritual death — being cut off from God forever. And everyone must die. You can either die alone or you can die in Jesus.[13]

For Jesus has died our death. And Jesus is God. I once remarked in a Bible class that when Jesus died, God died. "That bothers me," someone responded.

The death of Jesus always hits people that way, once they really understand who he is. And that's the way it should be. Surrounded by the antiseptic crosses of our jewelry, art and architecture we all need to recognize that there is something profoundly unsettling about the cross of Jesus Christ. "The message of the cross is foolishness to those who are perishing, but to us who are being saved it is the power of God" (1 Corinthians 1:18).

The cross is unsettling because it is God's drastic solution to our drastic problem. There he himself bore our sins in his body, and it killed him. You wouldn't expect God to work that way. You would never expect God to submit to suffering and death, but he did. And because he did, we have hope!

In his death Jesus Christ swallowed up our death, and rose again triumphantly to take all of the teeth out of the grave. In the promise of the resurrection, death loses its power. When we die with Jesus, we really live!

Wanted: dead and alive!

There is no sidestepping death. Everyone must die. It is the basic human dilemma. But the cross is God's great answer to our predicament. We needn't die alone. Jesus long ago died in our place, and that means that every baptized Christian dies in Jesus.

"Don't you know," St. Paul wrote (Romans 6:3) "that all of us who were baptized into Christ Jesus were baptized into his death?" Far from being some mere symbol of our dedication to Jesus, holy baptism is the God-appointed means of planting the cross of Jesus Christ squarely in the midst of our lives.

In our baptism Christ takes us in his arms, sins and all, and carries us into his own tomb to die with him. Death is always frightening. But this death is different, for when you die with Jesus, you also live with him. "If we have been united with him in his death, we will certainly also be united with him in his resurrection" (Romans 6:5).

That means that if we die in Jesus through our baptism, we also live in Jesus; a resurrection takes place. After baptism the person appears to everyone else to be the same human being, but not to God. The difference is that we have died and risen along with Christ: "We were therefore buried with him through baptism into death in order that, just as Christ was raised from the dead through the glory of the Father, we too may live a new life" (Romans 6:4).

After our burial with Christ in our baptism we are no longer the same person in God's sight. Our sins have been left behind in his tomb — the one place in all the universe that the Father will not look. And we have a new life through faith in him; it is the risen life of Jesus Christ!

> For we know that our old self was crucified with him so that the body of sin might be rendered powerless, that we should no longer be slaves to sin — because anyone who has died has been freed from sin. Now if we died with Christ, we believe that we will also live with him. (Romans 6:6-8)

Through death to life

So we see that the cross of Jesus is far more than a nice decoration or a theological concept. In fact, it is the central hinge around which all of faith revolves. At the cross the hidden God has opened up his very heart for all to see. In the death of Jesus — which is the death of God — with eyes of faith we see most clearly the Father's love. Baptized into that death, the cross takes on a whole new dimension. Now we can see that the only route to life is through death. And death is not to be feared, if it is the death of Jesus — for his death brings life!

That's the hardest thing to learn. We are always trying to avoid hardship, pain and death. Yet the cross of Jesus reveals to us that the only life worth living is a life which is given through death — the death of Jesus. There is no getting around the cross of Christ; the Christian life is always a life under the cross.

Life under the cross

We always carry around in our body the death of Jesus, so that the life of Jesus may also be revealed in our body. (2 Corinthians 4:10)

I mentioned that the sixteenth chapter of Matthew provides a framework in which we can understand the centrality of the cross. In fact, it helps us see the direct connection between the cross of Christ and the place of suffering in the life of the Christian. "If anyone would come after me," Jesus says, "he must deny himself and take up his cross and follow me" (v. 24).

This is not a subject most of us like to hear about; we're not much interested in suffering. We view suffering and pain as an unfortunate interruption in our otherwise trouble-free lives. It's very hard for us to understand how God could possibly be at work in the dark days of life.

A continuing danger

Jesus warned his disciples against "the yeast of the Pharisees and Sadducees" (v. 11). This was the mindset that looked for dramatic earthly evidence for spiritual reality. Peter fell victim to this mindset when he rejected God's plan to save the world through suffering and the cross. He thought it was all some horrible mistake. "Never, Lord!," he said. "This shall never happen to you!" (v. 22)

The yeast of the Pharisees and Sadducees is still very active in our own lives. You and I have a hard time understanding how God could actually be at work in our hardship, trial and pain.

The grand paradox

The risen and ascended Lord holds out this promise to his church of all time: "Be faithful, even to the point of death, and I will give you the crown of life" (Revelation 2:10). The crown sounds good; death is something else again. But there is only one route to the crown — through the cross!

Along with the privilege of discipleship comes an awesome responsibility: "Take up your cross," Jesus says, "and follow me." The cross, you see, is not just the unique way in which God saved the world. It stands as the continuing model for the Christian life until the end of time. There is no way around the cross.

A lot of us don't like to hear talk like that. Like Peter, we say "Never, Lord!" But along with Jesus comes his cross. There is no ignoring it and no side-stepping it. To avoid the cross is to risk eternal consequences: "Whoever wants to save his life will lose it" (Matthew 16:25).

The cross is intimately attached to the crown. Amazingly enough, when we undergo pain and suffering for Jesus' sake, we end up gaining: " . . . but whoever loses his life for me will find it" (Matthew 16:26). The life we lose in suffering is counterfeit. The life we find is the real thing.

The real me

I have already mentioned that every baptized Christian has experienced a death and resurrection. By being baptized into Christ his death and his life are now ours. Baptism plants us under the cross of Christ where he died our death, and it plants the cross squarely into our lives as we now live "in Christ." Christ is actually living out his life through us, the members of his body. This is why the Apostle Paul can define his life so dramatically:

> I have been crucified with Christ and I no longer live, but Christ lives in me. The life I live in the body, I live by faith in the Son of God, who loved me and gave himself for me. (Galatians 2:20)

An identity crisis

If we focus on our own track record, we will never make much progress in the Christian life; our sinful nature is very much alive. We know all too well the endless seesaw St. Paul wrote about in Romans 8:19: "For what I do is not the good I want to do; no, the evil I do not want to do — this I keep on doing."

This can be particularly frustrating to those who believe that Christians should generally be on top of things. With the power Jesus supplies, we're supposed to be making real progress over sin.

But what happens when I'm not? What happens when I find that sin is not very easily rooted out of my life? Then I've got a problem; a problem of identity. Maybe I'm not as committed as I ought to be. Maybe I've not turned my life over to Jesus completely. Worse yet, maybe I'm not a Christian: maybe I never really decided for Jesus in the first place!

St. Paul's answer to this quandary is as dramatic in power as it is striking in simplicity: Two forces are at work in my life. There is the sinful nature, which is a slave to sin, and there is the new man ("I myself"), which is a slave to God. My salvation does not depend on which force wins out in any given situation, but on the rescue already accomplished by God through Jesus Christ. That is why in the very midst of a battle with sin the apostle can exult in freedom from sin: "Therefore, there is now no condemnation for those who are in Christ Jesus" (Romans 8:1).

That's the key to my identity crisis: I am very much aware of my sinful thoughts and actions, but there's more here than meets the eye. The new me is unseen, hidden in Christ!

The hidden life

Everyone loves a good mystery — when it comes to entertainment, that is. In our own lives it is quite another story. We'd all much prefer to have things up front, straightforward and perfectly obvious. We operate very well with things we can see, measure and touch. Unseen things tend to bother us a lot.

Maybe that's why people keep wondering where in the world God is. They keep looking for evidence of the reality of God within range of their feelings and senses. We've already seen that God does not make himself known that way. Rather, he hides under lowly outward forms the better to reveal himself to us. This is a mystery, to be sure — but reality, nevertheless.

Just as God is hidden to the human senses, so also the Christian life is hidden. All we can see and sense is our sin and guilt. But that is not the whole picture. There has been a death and resurrection. It is Christ's death and resurrection, of course. But it is also ours. It's ours through baptism:

> ... you have been given fullness in Christ, who is the head over every power and authority ... having been buried with him in baptism and raised with him through your faith in the power of God, who raised him from the dead. When you were dead in your sins ... God made you alive with Christ. (Colossians 2:10,12,13)

Outward appearances don't tell the whole story. Looking at my own life I am only too aware of my sin and failure. But as far as God is concerned, my sinful nature is dead and gone. He sees only the new man in Christ — perfect, whole and complete. This is reality, but it is a hidden reality:

> For you died, and your life is now hidden with Christ in God. When Christ, who is your life, appears, then you also will appear with him in glory. (Colossians 3:3,4)

This calls for faith. Our real identity as new men and women in Christ will not be obvious until he comes again. When he appears, then our holiness and worth and value will be apparent to everyone —including us! But not yet. Until then we live by faith, recognizing that the Christian life is a hidden life. Just as God hides himself under lowly appearances, so also our real identity as sons and daughters of the King is hidden under a weak and sinful nature.

It's fruitless to go on tinkering with our life style, trying to transform it into conformity with God's will on our own. When you operate on a corpse you don't heal, you only discover the cause of death. God's plan for change in us goes to the heart of the matter. He deals with the cause, not the symptoms. He works on us daily with the same reality he accomplished when we were baptized: death and resurrection.

If the new man goes on rising, the sinful nature continually must go on dying. That's why the Christian life is a daily return to our baptism — a life lived under the cross, in partnership with Jesus.

A partnership in suffering

I mentioned that there is no way around the cross of Jesus. You can't have Jesus without it, for the cross is at the heart of God's plan to save the world. Jesus first had to suffer many things at the hands of the leaders in Jerusalem and be killed before he could rise again. (Matthew 16:21). God does not give life to the world except through death: the death of his Son.

So also the only way we grow as Christians is through death: the death of our sinful nature. Just as there is no way around the cross for our justification, there is also no way around the cross for our sanctification. "Take up your cross," Jesus says, "and follow me." This is not to be feared, since it is a partnership with Jesus. Still, it is a partnership in suffering.

We have a tendency to ignore the reality of suffering in the Christian life. It's often viewed as a slip-up, a glitch in the wonderful life God has planned for his people. Many Christians find it embarrassing to admit that things are tough. Some refuse to talk about it at all.

If Christians find it difficult to believe that God would deliberately hide himself under lowly disguise, it's downright shocking to discover that God expects us to suffer. This doesn't correspond with the picture of God we have in our mind. But this god, too, is an idol.

Just as we must destroy the false god who operates openly through human senses and intellect, so we also have to smash the idol of comfort and ease. This god doesn't exist. The real God is one who deliberately plans to work in our lives through suffering. We can see that when we look to the cross of Jesus Christ. You can't separate Jesus and his cross. To be in partnership with Jesus means to be in the partnership of his cross.

It's a package deal. To know Christ is always to know both the power of his resurrection *and* "the fellowship of sharing in his sufferings." (Philippians 3:10) To be co-heirs with Christ means that we not only inherit his glory, *but also* share in his sufferings (Romans 8:17).

There is a reason for this. We live in enemy-occupied territory. "Our struggle is not against flesh and blood . . . " (Ephesians 6:12). Christ is doing battle against Satan and his cohorts. As members of Christ's kingdom, we also draw enemy fire. "In this world you will have trouble," Jesus warns (John

141

16:33). The life of the Christian is a life under the cross.

But God uses the cross for a constructive purpose.

Demolition and reconstruction

Before a building can be erected, the old structure has to be torn down. In a remodeling project, old walls have to be removed before new ones can be put up. God is involved in a spiritual construction project; we " ... like living stones, are being built into a spiritual house to be a holy priesthood, offering spiritual sacrifices acceptable to God through Jesus Christ" (1 Peter 2:5).

This is an ongoing process; it is a case of already and not yet.[14] Christians are both saints and sinners. Already we have been given fullness in Christ; we are perfectly whole and complete through faith in him (Colossians 2:10-12). This is reality; but this reality is invisible. Our new nature is currently hidden with Christ in God (Colossians 3:3). He is now working in us "to will and to act according to his good purpose" (Philippians 2:13). But in order for him to fulfill his purpose in us, he must destroy our sinful nature. This is where the cross comes in.

God often uses suffering and pain to demolish our sinful nature in the process of building us up in Christ. In order for his life to be more and more a part of our life, he makes us partners with him in his death; and our sinful nature continually goes on dying:

> We always carry around in our body the death of Jesus, so that the life of Jesus may also be revealed in our body. For we who are alive are always being

given over to death for Jesus' sake, so that his life may be revealed in our mortal body . . . Therefore we do not lose heart. Though outwardly we are wasting away, yet inwardly we are being renewed day by day. (2 Corinthians 4:10,11,16)

This is how the cross works in the Christian life. There is no crossless Christ — there is no Easter without Good Friday. The risen Lord we preach is also "Christ crucified" (1 Corinthians 1:23). The life he offers to all was purchased and won by his death. The cross of Jesus is the means by which he gives life to the world.

For the Christian the cross is never merely an event in ancient history. In our baptism we were buried with Jesus into his death, which is the death of the cross. Now we live under the cross. But the way of the cross is the way to life. Rather than fleeing from suffering and pain, Jesus invites us to take up our cross and follow him. The only life we've got to lose is counterfeit; the life we gain is the real thing — it is the life he lives through us!

Pruning shears come before the harvest. Demolition comes before reconstruction. Already we are God's children by faith in Christ, but "what we will be has not yet been made known" (1 John 3:2).

Imagine yourself as a living house. God comes in to rebuild that house. At first, perhaps, you can understand what he is doing. He is getting the drains right and stopping the leaks in the roof and so on: you knew that those jobs needed doing and so you are not surprised. But presently he starts knocking the house about in a way that hurts abominably and does not seem to make sense. What on earth is he up to? The explanation is that he is building quite a different house from the one you thought of — throwing out a new wing here, putting on an extra floor there, running up towers, making courtyards. You thought you were going to be made into a decent little cottage: but he is building a palace. He intends to come and live in it himself.[15]

Prayer: battleground of the cross

If we hope for what we do not yet have, we wait for it patiently. In the same way, the Spirit helps us in our weakness. We do not know what we ought to pray, but the Spirit himself intercedes for us with groans that words cannot express. (Romans 8:25,26)

As we live under the cross, our search for God becomes more urgent. "Where in the world is God?" is no casual question to the man or woman facing despair, loneliness or terminal illness. We long for some contact with the living God. We want him to speak to us and bring meaning into a world which seems to have gone crazy. We would like some indication, some sign, that God is still on our side and that he is in control. We ask, "Why, God?" But no sign is given to us except the sign of Jonah.

We forget that God hides in order to make himself known. In a world in which we are bombarded by talk, we forget that God's silence is his most eloquent way of communicating with us. We keep listening for some word from him, but we forget that God has spoken most clearly in the cross of his Son. What he has said there is simply this, that there is nothing in all creation which will be able to separate us from his love.

If God is for us, who can be against us? He who did not spare his own Son, but gave him up for us all —how will he not also, along with him, graciously give us all things? (Romans 8:31,32)

144

This puts prayer in a whole different light. Whenever we pray expecting God to speak to us, we will be disappointed. He has already done that; he has given us his Word: "In these last days he has spoken to us by his Son" (Hebrews 1:2). If we ask for something more we're actually rejecting his Word and promise. Prayers which seek additional evidence from God are prayers of doubt, not of faith. But prayer under the cross is always the prayer of faith. "We fix our eyes not on what is seen, but on what is unseen" (2 Corinthians 4:18).

Prayer then becomes not a comfortable break from the trials of life, but the very place where we do battle against Satan, the world and our own sinful nature. Armed with our own inner resources and spiritual strength we're doomed to defeat. But God supplies the real equipment we need for this combat — the breastplate of righteousness, the shield of faith, the helmet of salvation, and his Word, which is the Spirit's sword (Ephesians 6:13ff). And over this battleground of prayer flies a victorious banner: the sign of the cross of Christ.

Life under the cross is a joyous life, for it is in our weakness that we can see the grace of Christ most clearly. That's why the most effective prayers are offered with empty hands. "God, have mercy on me, a sinner," the publican prayed (Luke 18:13). Humility, trials and faith all come together in prayer. We don't expect to hear God speak to us when we pray; he has already spoken in the cross. But prayer is where the Christian lives most intensively under the cross. We discover, as Jacob did, that it is when we wrestle with God that he blesses us most richly.

Dying to live

> May I never boast except in the cross of our Lord Jesus Christ, through which the world has been crucified to me, and I to the world. (Galatians 6:14)

Life under the cross sounds a bit morbid. At first glance it looks as though God wants to turn us all into masochists, people who find a perverse pleasure in pain. But there is nothing pleasurable about the cross. The cross of Jesus was an instrument of torture and death. It was there he suffered and died, and it was a humiliating and agonizing death.

Yet it was because he humbled himself all the way to the death of the cross that he has been exalted to the highest place and has been given the name which is above every name (Philippians 2:8,9). In his death he has destroyed death; by his cross he has won the victory!

This changes the picture entirely. Rather than running away from suffering and pain, the Christian finds joy in the cross. This joy, however, is not because of the pain; it is joy found in the grace and mercy of God. In the cross of Christ God revealed the fullness of his love for us, and in the crosses he places before us he draws us closer to him.

Today's Evangelicals often have difficulty with suffering and hardship. Used to looking for God to work in obvious and evidential ways, they can't comprehend how God could use sorrow and pain to demonstrate his love. This isn't surprising; if you have your eyes only on the heights you will miss God where he is usually at work — in the depths. Luther understood that suffering, pain and death are precisely the locations where God is often to be found in the word of his gospel:

A theologian of the cross (that is, one who speaks of the crucified and hidden God), teaches that punishments, crosses and death are the most precious treasury of all and the most sacred relics which the Lord of this theology himself has consecrated and blessed, not alone by the touch of his most holy flesh but also by the embrace of his exceedingly holy and divine will, and he has left these relics here to be kissed, sought after and embraced. Indeed, fortunate and blessed is he who is considered by God to be so worthy that these treasures of the relics of Christ should be given to him; rather, who understands that they are given to him.[16]

We must be clear on one thing: there is no virtue in suffering. Humiliation and pain earn us no favor with God. He takes no delight in our sorrow. There is joy under the cross because that's where we meet God. We humbly accept our suffering not because God rewards our humility, but because his love and grace can only be received when our hands are emptied of all idols and our sinful pride is crushed. The cross is the scalpel of God's mercy; he uses pain to crucify our sinful nature and give us real life instead — the life we have already been given by our baptism into Christ.

Now we see that our sufferings are signs of God's presence in our lives. They are no more convincing to human reason than was the cross of Jesus, but they are no less real. Those who understand the sign of Jonah recognize the cross as a badge of honor — it is the mark of God's ownership.

The apostles left the Sanhedrin, rejoicing because they had been counted worthy of suffering disgrace for the Name. (Acts 5:42)

Finally, let no one cause me trouble, for I bear on my body the marks of Jesus. (Galatians 6:17)

147

Finders may be keepers in the world's point of view, but Jesus figures things differently. In wanting to keep your life, you lose it. In losing, you win. In dying, you live. This is the life style he holds out for us. It's not really a life style at all; it is actually Christ's life — the life he lives through us. It is a joyous life. And from beginning to end it's always the same life: a life under the cross.

The real thing

This life is not hypothetical, it is an actual reality God offers us in the person of Jesus Christ, his Son. God still comes to our world today as he did in the incarnation and the cross, through channels which are tangible, though hidden and lowly. We call these channels the sacraments. We can't really afford to overlook them if we want to know where in the world God is.

6

CHRIST IN ACTION: THE SACRAMENTS, ABSOLUTION AND WORSHIP

Beyond all question, the mystery of godliness is great:
He appeared in a body,
was vindicated by the Spirit,
was seen by angels,
was preached among the nations,
was believed on in the world,
was taken up in glory.
(1 Timothy 3:16)

God with us

I mentioned that this book is a kind of pilgrimage toward the Lutheran heritage. This next stop along the way is one of the most familiar, and yet in many ways one of the most confusing.

The sacraments at first glance seem to be a curiosity — like old family heirlooms in a house full of modern furniture. Their chief value seems to be in their age, and not in their practicality. No one would like to throw them out since they've been in the family for so long, but they don't really seem to fit, either! But the sacraments, far from being relics of a by-gone era in church history, are actually part and parcel of the Christian gospel for all time.

If the pressing issue today is finding out where in the world God is, there is nothing more practical than understanding what he intends to accomplish through the sacraments. Along the way on this journey I have emphasized that you can't find God in your own heart or emotions. Rather, the reality of God and the power of his presence is only found in the person and work of Jesus.

In every case in God's dealings with mankind, it is God who makes the first move. This is true also in the sacraments. Baptism and the Lord's Supper are not intrusions into the worship service; properly understood, they are God's intrusions into our lives! In fact, they are based upon and extend God's intrusion into this world of ours in the person of his Son.

The impossible reality

If you really want to understand the sacraments, you have to begin with the incarnation of the Son of God. Since the Scriptures teach that Jesus is truly God and truly man at one and the same time, there is no reason to doubt that physical elements could be vehicles of spiritual reality.

Human logic has a problem with this. Reason can never grasp how the finite could possibly be capable of the infinite. Christians, however, always need to take their stand on faith rather than reason. It was faith, not reason, that led the shepherds to the lowly cattle shed and faith which led them to see the Lord of all the universe wrapped in swaddling cloths.

It isn't because the Lutheran church can't bear to throw out old pre-Reformation heirlooms that it hangs on to the sacraments. Rather, our church is sacramental because we take the incarnation very seriously. If, in the person of Jesus Christ, God died and man now is ascended to the Father's right hand in glory, anything is possible! Instead of forcing the Bible to undergo the scrutiny of human logic, Lutherans prefer to bow the knee in acknowledging the mystery of the Christian faith.

The mystery of the gospel

The scriptural key to unlocking a sacramental understanding is the New Testament Greek word *mysterion*, "mystery." This is the word, translated *sacramentum* in the Latin Bible, which has come into our language as "sacrament." In the verse at the head of this section, St. Paul calls the confession of the church, its whole body of doctrine, "the mystery of godliness" (1 Timothy 3:16). In his letter to the Colossians, he calls the Christian gospel "the mystery that has been kept hidden for ages and generations, but is now disclosed to the saints" (Colossians 1:26). By using the term he wishes to emphasize not just the complexity of the gospel, but also its dynamic power.

I have already shown how God reveals himself by hiding in the cross of his Son. The message of God's salvation in Jesus Christ always works that way; it is both hidden and revealed. It is hidden because it is beyond reach of human reason, but it is revealed through God's self-disclosure in his Son. Paradoxically, though he is unknowable in his majesty, God has made himself known to us in his grace.

Who's the actor?

Most Evangelical Christians see the sacraments as "ordinances" — actions which God has commanded us to do. Communion thus becomes our way of fulfilling Jesus' will that he be memorialized in this meal until he returns. Baptism is understood to be the act by which the believer confirms his prior decision to accept Jesus; by submitting to baptism he publicly demonstrates his commitment to Jesus as Savior and Lord.

The issue here goes to the heart of the gospel. Who is at work in God's relationship with human beings: man or God? Are the sacraments our offerings to God, or are they God's offerings to us? Most Evangelicals hold the first view. Robert Webber describes that view in his remarkable personal account of his switch from Fundamentalism to a sacramental church:

> I had looked on the sacraments as *my* sign of faith directed toward God. My impression was that I could show God that I loved him by being baptized and by eating the bread and drinking the wine. But the early church, and with them the Reformers, presented the sacraments as God's signs, not ours. In and through them God actively conveys himself and his grace. They are his signs, and as I participate in faith, my relationship with him is established, repaired, and maintained.[1]

If we understand how God works in the incarnation of his Son and in his cross, we can see that he works in the same way through the sacraments. God is the actor; he has made the first move. Though we could not ascend to heaven, he has come to earth. What we could never reach through our senses, God has placed within reach of our senses — first in the incarnation of his Son, then in the sacraments. What we could never arrive at through human logic, God gives us power to believe.

Logic and mystery

The inability of the human mind to come into contact with God outside of his self-revelation goes against our grain. We would like to think that we are in the driver's seat when getting in touch with God. We prefer to believe that there is no secret of the universe which cannot be unlocked by the human brain. Consequently, we find large segments of American Protestantism have rejected the very concept of "mystery."

> To a society that has staked its spirituality on *scientia* rather than *sapientia*, knowledge instead of wisdom, mystery must remain the enemy. . . . mystery is ultimately doomed, we think. Given enough time and money, our technology will reveal all secrets, from the farthest quasar to the nearest sub-atomic particle. The very notion that there is something, anything, that by its very nature *cannot* be known to us inside the prison of our five senses, whips us into a fury.[2]

But rather than following human reason, it is crucial to let God be God; to take him at his word regarding the reality of sacramental power. After all, the very wisdom of God is hidden in a mystery[3] — the mystery of God made flesh, which is also the profound mystery of his cross.

Outward action or inner experience?

Evangelicals have tended to see sacramental churches as dead churches because they rely merely on outward acts. Genuine commitment and exciting power, they contend, are to be found in the inner experience of faith. Nothing could be farther from the truth. Instead of detracting from sincerity of faith and depth of commitment to our Lord, a proper understanding of the power of the sacraments enhances the new life in Christ. These outward acts are the very means by which God works on our inner experience. Luther writes:

> The inward experience follows and is effected by the outward. God has determined to give the inward to no one except through the outward. For he wants to give no one the Spirit or faith outside the outward Word and sign instituted by him, as he says in Luke 16, "Let them hear Moses and the prophets." Accordingly Paul can call baptism a "washing of regeneration." And the oral gospel "is the power of God for salvation to every one who has faith."[4]

If we want to know where in the world God is, this understanding of the "mystery of the gospel" is central. Here in tangible human elements — the oral word, the water of baptism, and the bread and wine of the holy supper, Christ extends to us the benefits of his saving work. Sacramental action is no mechanistic, robot-like activity, of course. The benefits attached to these earthly elements by the power of God's Word are to be accepted in faith.[5] Still, the glorious reality is that in these external means we meet Christ. And through these external means he offers us the benefits of his saving work!

A space/time warp

A favorite gospel hymn asks the wistful question: "Were you there when they crucified my Lord?" Unfortunately time and space remove us from that pivotal sacrifice by which God's wrath was removed. And we are also separated from the historical event of the resurrection in which Christ triumphed over sin, death and hell. Nevertheless, twentieth century Christians can claim the benefits of that saving action — not by ascending to heaven in prayer and meditation, nor by descending to find God in the inner workings of the renewed heart, but by Christ's condescension to us in his baptismal washing and in his supper.

Remember, this is Christ at work! Christ conveys his power to us in these sacraments, and here he offers the benefits of his saving work for faith to grasp. Through these channels his spiritual power intersects with our material world. In the reception of the sacraments, the barriers of time and space are removed, and we are made contemporaries with those who stood at the foot of the cross and those who sat at table in the upper room.

The sure foundation

If you and I are to have any certainty in the Christian faith, it must be grounded on the objective promises of the external word of the gospel. The experience of faith is a result, not the cause, of our salvation. The real experience which saves is the experience of Jesus in enduring the Father's wrath on the cross. In his death on the cross, he has triumphed over all the demonic forces (Colossians 2:15). In what appeared to be complete and total defeat at Calvary, he has won the final victory. The message of the cross may look like foolishness to the world, but to those who belong to Christ by faith that message is the very power of God for salvation (1 Corinthians 1:18, Romans 1:16). "This is the testimony," St. John wrote, "that God has given us eternal life, and that this life is *in his Son*" (1 John 5:11). That same divine life which gives life to the world (John 1:4; 6:33) is made available to us in the sacraments.

Born again

"Don't you know," St. Paul writes to the Romans, "that all of us who were baptized into Christ Jesus were baptized into his death? We were therefore buried with him through baptism into death in order that, just as Christ was raised from the dead through the glory of the Father, we too may live a new life" (Romans 6:3,4).

With all of its talk about the born-again experience, Evangelicalism largely fails to see the real new birth. It is a birth which Jesus explains takes place by the power of the Holy Spirit working through water (John 3:5). By this washing of rebirth and renewal of the Holy Spirit (Titus 3:5) we are brought into contact with Christ and joined with him in his death (Romans 6). Now the Father considers his death as our death. Our sins are totally paid for, and we are joined with Christ in his resurrection.

The baptismal life: Christ in me

This means that there is now a whole new dimension to the Christian life. Now as we live in the real world, Christ actually lives within us (Galatians 2:20). The new life we live is really Christ's life; after all, we have been joined with him by baptism into his resurrection (Romans 6:5). Now, since we have been raised with Christ and he is actually living within us, we set our sights on heavenly matters, where Christ reigns in ascended glory (Colossians 3:1,2).

Our union with Christ by baptism is a merging into his death as well as his resurrection:

> Undoubtedly the baptism into Christ (Galatians 3:27; Romans 6:3; Colossians 2:11) at the same time produces an emerging into the inmost, personal life communion with the risen Lord, who thus becomes a present active possession, but we dare never forget that it is a union with One who has been exalted and glorified, who bears in his body the wounds of the cross, in whom is life and who has given that life for us on the cross. It is our justification on the basis of the death of Christ and not the renewal that is begun in the sacrament, that gives the act of baptism its character of irrevocable validity.[6]

Baptism is a continual reminder that God does not leave us to fend for ourselves in the Christian life. We say with the apostle Paul: "I live, yet not I, but Christ lives in me" (Galatians 2:20). We are not left to our own devices in doing battle against our sinful nature, Satan and the world around us.

Baptism is the sign of God's promise. The promise is just this: we are dead and alive. Our sinful self is dead and buried with Christ. We are a new creation, risen with him by faith to live a new life. And that new baptismal life is nothing less than the life which Christ lives out through us. "For as many of you as were baptized into Christ have put on Christ" (Galatians 3:27[RSV]).

The forgotten reality

This truth is a hidden truth. The baptismal life is, after all, a hidden life. It is because of our baptismal burial with Christ (Colossians 2:12) that the apostle can say rather bluntly: "For you died, and your life is now hidden with Christ in God" (Colossians 3:3). Not only is this life invisible to people around us, but the reality of Christ's operation in us by our baptism sometimes escapes us as well. In the eloquent prayer in his letter to the Ephesian Christians, St. Paul requests that God would enable them to see with their hearts what they could not see with their eyes:

> I pray also that the eyes of your heart may be enlightened in order that you may know the hope to which he has called you, the riches of his glorious inheritance in the saints, and his incomparably great power for us who believe. (Ephesians 1:18,19)

The power at work in the Christian life, the apostle writes to the Ephesians, is the very same power the Father "exerted in Christ when he raised him from the dead and seated him at his right hand in the heavenly realms" (1:20).

The Jesus connection

By our baptism, you see, God works in a parallel fashion in our lives; what he did in raising Christ from the dead he does in bringing us from death to life. For every one of us were dead in our transgressions and sins (2:1), under the wrath of God by nature (2:3). The thing to do with a dead body is to bury it. And that's exactly what God did. He buried us along with Jesus in his tomb by our baptism. But the tomb of Jesus stands empty. And baptism is our link not only with the death of Jesus, but also with his resurrection. Therefore we are risen and alive too — in Christ!

The power of baptism for the Christian life is simply this: the power at work in Jesus himself. This is how our sin is erased and we stand forgiven before God, for just as the Father "raised him from the dead" (1:20), so he has "raised us up with Christ" (2:6) by our baptism. But our baptismal connection with Jesus also brings with it his power for living day by day: just as the Father "seated him at his right hand in the heavenly realms" (1:20), so also he has "seated us with him in the heavenly realms" (2:6).

So what?

No wonder we run into problems trying to live the Christian life under our own steam. "You died," is the message our baptism gives us (Colossians 3:3). Dead people don't accomplish much. But we have a new life — Jesus Christ himself is alive in us by our baptism. Now we live each day in the power of the crucified and risen Lord — which is precisely the power of our baptism.

Luther underscored the practical implications of this power for the everyday life of the Christian in his *Small Catechism*:

What does such baptizing with water indicate?

It indicates that the Old Adam in us should by daily contrition and repentance be drowned and die with all sins and evil desires, and that a new man should daily emerge and arise to live before God in righteousness and purity forever.

Where is this written?

St. Paul writes in Romans chapter six: We were therefore buried with him through baptism into death in order that, just as Christ was raised from the dead through the glory of the Father, we too may live a new life.[7]

This is the new life we have by our baptism. It is the new life of Jesus Christ himself. That's why the Christian life is never merely the Christian in action; it is Christ in action!

"Remember when ... ?"

For most of American Protestantism the sacrament of the altar is primarily a way to arouse memories of Jesus or a fellowship meal in which the congregation shares in an act of Christian hospitality. Bruce Blackie's critique of mainline Protestantism could easily apply as well to much of Evangelicalism:

> The sacrament, to most people, means nothing in itself or apart from the mood of sentiment that it creates. The dying and risen Christ, the concept of the universal church, and even a sense of dinner fellowship with other church members elude the parishioner as he partakes of diced Bond bread and a tiny sip of Welch's grape juice.[8]

The Lord's Supper is again best understood in light of the incarnation. Since Jesus has taken on human flesh without sacrificing any of his divinity, he is now able to distribute that same flesh in connection with the earthly elements of the sacrament:

> It is taught among us that the true body and blood of Christ are really present in the Supper of our Lord under the form of bread and wine and are there distributed and received. The contrary doctrine is therefore rejected. (Augsburg Confession, Article X. "The Holy Supper of our Lord")

What did Jesus mean?

Down through the centuries great controversy has swirled around the words "This is my body; this is my blood." What exactly did Jesus mean by these words? Some have held that he meant something like: "This *represents* my body . . . my blood." Certainly Jesus often does use picture language in his teaching.

The setting, however, indicates something different. Jesus gathered with his disciples "on the night when he was betrayed," St. Paul reminds us, stressing the sober mood of the evening (1 Corinthians 11:25). This was the last Passover he was to celebrate with his friends. He informs them, "I have eagerly desired to eat this Passover with you before I suffer" (Luke 22:15). This was neither the time nor the place for picture language. He uses none of the kind of language he used in parables. ("The kingdom of heaven is like, etc.") He speaks in straightforward, simple, declarative sentences. Rather than explain them another way, it's up to us to be faithful to his words: "This is my body; this is my blood . . . do this in remembrance of me" (Matthew 26:26-28; Mark 14:22-24; Luke 22:19,20; 1 Corinthians 11:23-25). In each of the four locations where Jesus is quoted, he identifies his blood in the supper with the new testament.

Testament and seal

The word "testament" was well-known to the men Jesus spoke to that night of his betrayal. To them it recalled the granting of the covenant at Sinai where God's agreement with his people was signed, sealed and delivered in animal blood.

A blood sacrifice

That scene is recorded in Exodus 24. After hearing the oral rendition of God's law, the Israelites said unanimously: "Everything the Lord has said we will

161

do." After Moses had written down the words of God, he prepared an altar and sacrificed bulls to the Lord, retaining the blood of the animals and dividing it into two parts. Half of it he kept in bowls while he sprinkled the other half on the altar. This constituted God's good intentions toward his people and his covenant offer to them. When Moses had read the terms of the agreement to them (in the form of the Book of the Covenant), the Israelites again responded: "We will do everything the Lord has said; we will obey." Now the testament was sealed; the blood which had been set aside in the bowls was sprinkled over the people. "This," Moses informed them, "is the blood of the covenant that the Lord has made with you in accordance with all these words."

The civilized mind is revolted at the sight of a comparatively small amount of blood. At Sinai there was blood everywhere: on the altar, in the bowls, and then on the people! The purpose of this gory mess was to vividly portray to the people exactly what was happening to them. God was establishing a covenant with them. Since the animals had been offered to him, it was his blood. God was sprinkling his blood on his people to show them that there was an intimate bond between them. To this day we have the expression "blood brothers." It stems from the practice of two men pledging their life-long friendship by cutting their flesh and mingling their blood. The blood becomes the bond between them.

The night before his crucifixion Jesus established his last will and testament for his church. It was signed and sealed not with a notary's signature, but with his own blood, just as the testament at Sinai had been long before.

The great liberation

Jesus utilized the elements of the Passover meal, which was itself rich with the memory of God's miraculous deliverance of his people from bondage and death to glorious freedom from slavery. In Egypt God had saved his people from the plague of the death of the first-born by prescribing the death of a lamb on their behalf. The lamb's blood on their doorposts would deliver them from death; God would "pass over" them on his deadly mission. Each year Israel was to observe a feast as a living memorial to their miraculous deliverance:

> And when your children ask you, "What does this ceremony mean to you?" then tell them, "It is the Passover sacrifice to the Lord, who passed over the houses of the Israelites in Egypt and spared our homes when he struck down the Egyptians." (Exodus 12:26,27)

Some fourteen centuries later the true Lamb of Israel, about to shed his blood for the salvation of the whole world, took the bread and wine of the Passover and said to his friends in the upper room: "Take, eat, this is my body. . . . Take, drink, this is the new testament in my blood."

This room was more loaded with blood imagery than the altar at Sinai, dripping with the blood of the bulls. Here was the Lamb of God, about to offer his own blood on the altar of the cross, now distributing that same blood to his disciples. Like the blood of the bulls at Sinai, it was the sign and seal of an agreement. Unlike the animal blood, this was the very blood of the Son of God, which cleanses us from all sin (1 John 1:7).

163

A real reality

The purpose of this extended historical narrative is to help us understand Jesus' words in his supper. When the setting of the text is considered within the context of: (1) the Passover meal; (2) the betrayal of Jesus, the true Lamb of God, for his death; and (3) the connection of the "new" testament with the Sinai covenant; the meaning is quite clear.

Jesus actually means to distribute to his church the very body and blood with which he made satisfaction for the sins of the world. It is therefore a sign and seal of the forgiveness of our sins and the continual reminder that God includes us in his kingdom.

The value of the sacrament of the altar can hardly be overestimated for anyone who wants to know where God is at work in this world. From his Father's right hand in glory, Jesus continues to distribute to people of every age the very same body and blood with which he earned their salvation. Here again time and space are removed, and we join with the saints of all time in common celebration of the testament established once and for all at the cross outside Jerusalem. In his holy supper, Jesus gives us reality, not symbol.

> The old covenant became valid and effective only by a bloody yielding to death, so the new covenant can be realized only if he [Jesus], as both the Victim and the Priest, gives himself to God as a sacrifice of reconciliation. As the One who actually suffers death (and does not merely talk spectacularly about the symbolism of death) he gives his congregation not merely a sign of his death but the actual result of his death, which is the reconciliation of the world and the gift of a new relationship of peace with God that has been purchased through sacrifice.[9]

Earthly experience/heavenly reality

It is time to develop a practice of the Lord's Supper which is consistent with a New Testament understanding of it; which helps people to grasp the full dimension of its application to their lives. Lutheran Christians often look elsewhere for spiritual food because they haven't been taught to see the rich banquet spread by the Lord of the church in his supper. All too often they see it as just another demand on their time on busy Sunday mornings.

Properly understood, the sacrament of the altar can be an effective experiential event.[10] While other forms of piety attempt to climb to heaven by achieving a certain state of spirituality, Lutheran piety centers around the reality of Christ present with his church in his Word and sacrament.

Looking in the right places

An assault on heaven is a doomed journey; our sinful nature cuts us off from God. But, thankfully, he has made the contact with us in his incarnate Son. Still today, through his Word and sacraments, he stoops to come to us in connection with the lowly and common elements of water, bread and wine.

If we want to see God at work in our world, let's stay away from the "never-never land" of subjective emotions and the fluctuations of the renewed heart. Let's find him where he has promised to meet us! Just as only the shepherds with their eyes of faith could see anything extraordinary in the manger at Bethlehem, so those who humbly bow at Christ's word find him in the lowly elements of ordinary bread and wine.

165

Christ in action: absolution

> I tell you the truth, whatever you bind on earth will be bound in heaven, and whatever you loose on earth will be loosed in heaven. . . . For where two or three come together in my name, there am I with them. (Matthew 18:18,20)

> It is taught among us that private absolution should be retained and not allowed to fall into disuse.
> (Augsburg Confession: Article XI. "Confession")

Possibility or reality?

In their important early study of the rise of modern Evangelicalism, Wells and Woodbridge make the following observation about the movement's dramatic switch in direction:

> In the reformers' formulation and well into the nineteenth century, evangelicalism was God's way of salvation, not only in the offering of it to men but in the applying of it to their hearts as well. Last century, however, the evangel began to be seen more as the divine offer of grace and not so much as the divine application of grace.[11]

Christians today are concerned with one central issue: Where in the world is God? How can I be reassured of his love in the face of the complexities and traumas of my life? As we can see from the above quote, the historic answer of the heirs of the reformation has been: *in the gospel*. Modern Evangelicals, however, do not see the gospel as the means of applying the love of God to the sinner as much as they see it as information about the love of God. The gospel is understood to be an "offer of grace," rather than the "application of grace." It has no power itself, the power is in your decision to accept it.

166

In contrast, the Lutheran church has always stressed that the gospel is both the offer of grace and the means of its application. After dealing with the central doctrine of justification by grace through faith, that is, that God will consider our faith in Jesus as righteousness, the Augsburg Confession turns immediately to the application of salvation:

> To obtain such faith God instituted the office of the ministry, that is, provided the gospel and the sacraments. Through these, as through means, he gives the Holy Spirit, who works faith, when and where he pleases, in those who hear the gospel. And the gospel teaches that we have a gracious God, not by our own merits but by the merit of Christ, when we believe this. (Augsburg Confession: Article V. "The Office of the Ministry")

Gospel: history or power?

I have already demonstrated that Evangelical Christians today tend to see the gospel as mere historical data. Accordingly, if you want to take advantage of this information you do it by making a decision to commit yourself to Jesus. The Bible has a dramatically different view; here the shoe is on the other foot. God takes the initiative, just as he did in the incarnation of his Son.

The gospel is not just historical information, but the living power of the living God. Jesus said: "The words which I have spoken to you are Spirit and they are life" (John 6:63). No wonder then that Paul saw the gospel not as a static message but as life-giving power: "I am not ashamed of the gospel of Christ, for it is the power of God for salvation to everyone who believes" (Romans 1:16).

167

Christ in Action:

A *personal gospel*

Jesus noted that the gospel would be preached in all the world as a testimony to all nations (Matthew 24:14). But his gospel is not intended only for general consumption. The living Lord has also instructed his church to apply it individually. On the night after his resurrection from the dead, Jesus said to his disciples: "Receive the Holy Spirit. If you forgive anyone his sins, they are forgiven; if you do not forgive them, they are not forgiven" (John 20:22,23).

No human being can forgive sins, of course. Jesus, however, has empowered his church with his own authority: "As the Father has sent me, I am sending you" (John 20:21). He has therefore delegated to his human followers the power to announce to penitent sinners not just the possibility of forgiveness, but forgiveness itself. Whether spoken publicly or in private, the forgiveness verbalized by a spokesman for Jesus is actually his own forgiveness: "If you forgive anyone his sins, they are forgiven."

Accordingly Luther included in his catechism, as one of the chief parts of Christian doctrine, a section titled "Confession."

> *What is Confession?*
>
> Confession has two parts. First, that we confess our sins, and Second, that we receive absolution, that is, forgiveness, from the pastor as from God Himself, not doubting, but firmly believing that by it our sins are forgiven before God in heaven.

In order to help people learn how to confess to their pastor, Luther also included a sample order for personal confession and absolution.

168

Confession to a pastor

Recent generations of Lutherans have so neglected private confession that it is for all practical purposes dead. We can only hope for a resuscitation — out of faithfulness to the Lord who instituted it, to be sure, but also out of concern for the deeply wounded and scarred consciences of Christians doing battle against sin in our day.

Current pastoral care for the troubled sinner consists of an intensive series of counseling sessions. Such counsel may indeed be necessary in order for the person to escape sin's "fallout." It does nothing, however, for the guilt of sin.

People hounded by guilt are extremely attracted to revivalism. Here the troubled sinner is told to pray and meditate on his inner feelings of the grace of God; maybe he has fallen from grace (particularly if he comes from a "dead church") and needs a fresh experience of conversion in order to rid himself of guilt. When he finally comes to the point of total surrender, he will see the subjective responses of the new life beginning in his feelings and actions. When he has these inner feelings, he can be sure that God has forgiven him.

The Bible has another view. In connection with his struggle against guilt and sin, St. Paul exclaims in anguish: "What a wretched man I am! Who will rescue me from this body of death? Thanks be to God — through Jesus Christ our Lord!" (Romans 7:24,25) Here the answer is not reform, but rescue. The reform will follow.[12]

Where else can we look for the word of forgiveness than where God has promised to give it? Rather than search inside for feelings that show I am in a state of grace, it's important to listen to God speak. In holy absolution he speaks loud and clear. What could be more clear than the audible word of the gospel pronounced by Christ's servant in his name and in his place?

The time has come to begin restoring the practice of private confession and absolution to the life of the church. We can learn by the example of the churches of the Reformation.[13] There must be patient teaching and loving invitation, not compulsion. Then people will respond. Christian people always respond to the gospel, Luther reminds us:

> When I urge you to go to confession, I am simply urging you to be a Christian. If I bring you to this point, I have also brought you to confession. Those who really want to be good Christians, free from their sins, and happy in their conscience, already have the true hunger and thirst. They snatch at the bread just like a hunted hart, burning with heat and thirst, as Psalm 42:2 says, "As a hart longs for flowing streams, so longs my soul for thee, O God."[14]

Clubbing the serpent

This ministry is effective. I know; I've seen it in action. It's thrilling to see what happens in the confidential setting of confession as Christians wounded by sin and guilt are able to unload the sin that's been haunting them. "The serpent must stick its head out of its hole in order for it to be clubbed," Bonhoeffer reminds us.[15] This is more than getting something "off your chest." This is a confrontation with the poison and filth of sin. It's actually a kind of death. In fact, it is a return to baptism; it's a renewal of the death we died there to sin and a renewal of the resurrection we experienced there with Jesus Christ.

Reality, not possibility

Where is God when I'm hurting? This is the issue for people who are struggling with the pain of sin and guilt. The standard approach today is inadequate. We can do more than give biblical examples of people who triumphed over sin. We can do more than talk about "surrender." We can do more than provide how-to lists for living the "victorious life." Sin kills. And corpses don't triumph or surrender or live victorious lives. Remorseful sinners need rescue before reform. They need resurrection before rehabilitation. And this is exactly what Christ brings to the sinner in the word of his gospel absolution through the mouth of the pastor.

What a privilege it is for God's servant to look a Christian brother or sister in the eye and deal openly and honestly with the horror of his or her sin in the power of the gospel of the Lord Jesus Christ! "If the Son sets you free," Jesus said, "you will be free indeed" (John 8:36).

And Jesus still sets people free. He sets them free by the word of his gospel. This isn't just potential forgiveness; this is actual forgiveness itself. No more "if only . . . " games. This is real. In personal confession and absolution Jesus Christ still sets people free.

Confession to a neighbor

Pastors, as shepherds of their congregations, are charged to feed and care for their spiritual flocks.

171

Therefore they bear the prime responsibility for hearing confession and pronouncing absolution. The Bible indicates, however, that the practice is not limited to pastoral care: "Confess your sins to each other . . . " (James 5:16). There is a place for confession to one's neighbor as well as one's pastor. Just as all Christians witness to the gospel, while only pastors are called to proclaim it publicly, so also every Christian has the privilege of speaking the gospel to wounded consciences:

> For when we have laid bare our consciences to our brother and privately made known to him the evil that lurked within, we receive from our brother's lips the word of comfort spoken by God himself. And, if we accept this in faith, we find peace in the mercy of God speaking to us through our brother.[16]

There's a lot of talk these days about "discipling" Christians — training them to reach greater maturity as disciples, or followers, of the Lord Jesus. Typically this is to happen by developing close, trusting friendships with one or two fellow Christians in an atmosphere of mutual accountability. There is a crying need for such friendships; I have already commented on the isolation and loneliness in which most Christians live today. But we need more from our Christian brother or sister than sympathy or good advice!

God at work

In the isolation and loneliness of our world, what we really cry out for is love — no ordinary love, but the love of God. The really extraordinary thing is that God uses fellow Christians to make his love known to us:

This is love: not that we loved God, but that he loved us and sent his Son as an atoning sacrifice for our sins. Dear friends, since God so loved us, we also ought to love one another. No one has ever seen God; but if we love each other, God lives in us and his love is made complete in us. (1 John 4:10-12)

God reveals his love in only one place — the word of his gospel. That word, however, comes to us not only in preaching, sacraments and absolution, but also through interaction with Christian friends:

[The gospel] offers counsel and help against sin in more than one way, for God is surpassingly rich in his grace: First, through the spoken word, by which the forgiveness of sin (the peculiar function of the gospel) is preached to the whole world; second, through baptism; third, through the holy sacrament of the altar; fourth, through the power of keys; and finally, through the mutual conversation and consolation of brethren. Matthew 18:20, "Where two or three are gathered," etc.[17]

The encouraging word

This brings a whole new dimension to Christian friendship. One of the reasons loneliness has become an epidemic in our age is that people have learned to live behind masks. "He who is alone with his sin is utterly alone," Bonhoeffer wrote.[18] There is no reason to go on living with that kind of loneliness, for when Christians are able to take off their masks in each other's presence and confront the ugliness and pain of their sin, there is healing and peace. It is the peace of Jesus Christ, and it comes in the word of his gospel through the voice of our Christian friend.

. . . one humbles himself before the other, one comforts the other, one fittingly bears the burden and

173

weakness of the other. Together they are strengthened, empowered and grounded in the genuine unity of weary and sinburdened hearts, a unity which is found in him who justifies the ungodly out of grace.

Fortunate is that person who has a brother or two with whom he has such a bond of confession and honesty; there sins will decrease, and if one does fall, there are people who with a gentle spirit help to set him right again:

Two are better than one,
because they have a good return for their work:
If one falls down, his friend can help him up.
But pity the man who falls and has no one to help him
    up!
(Ecclesiastes 4:9,10)[19]

Christ in action: Worship

After this I looked and there before me was a great multitude that no one could count from every nation, tribe, people and language, standing before the throne and in front of the Lamb. They were wearing white robes and were holding palm branches in their hands. And they cried out in a loud voice:
Salvation belongs to our God,
who sits on the throne,
and to the Lamb!
... They fell down on their faces before the throne and worshiped God.
(Revelation 7:9-11)

Praise the Lord, O my soul;
all my inmost being, praise his holy name!
(Psalm 103:1)

Greener pastures?

The common criticism leveled against liturgical churches is that they are cold and unfeeling. "I left that church," the saying goes, "because I wasn't being fed."

No greater indictment could be leveled against any church calling itself Christian. The Good Shepherd, who has given his life for the church (John 10:11) has specifically left instructions for the care and feeding of his sheep (John 21:15-17). Pastors, whose very name means "shepherd," are charged to "keep watch over yourselves and all the flock of which the Holy Spirit has made you overseers. Be shepherds of the church of God, which he bought with his own blood" (Acts 20:28). The faithful church will always see that the flock is fed, not with junk food, but with the solid nourishment of the Word and sacrament.

What people mean when they say they're not being fed, however, usually has less to do with spiritual nourishment than it does with spiritual taste buds. What they really mean is that they're looking for a different emotional climate. In our consumer society, Christian people tend to shop for the church where they find the right mix of preaching and worship to suit their tastes. Here style is often more important than content, atmosphere more important than doctrine. A church with an appealing style of worship will be more likely to attract the attention of the Evangelical "shopper" in today's church market.

Pop music

Evangelical churches are quite adept at finding worship styles that please their constituency. Popular musical styles are used, and on Sunday morning in most Evangelical churches of America people can hear the same music they've been listening to all week, with sacred lyrics added. The Christian church has often borrowed musical settings from the culture it lives in. The hymns of Martin Luther are a case in point. Many of his original hymns are set to tunes from the popular music of his day. "Why should the devil have all the good music?" was his rather pointed question; one which modern Christians would do well to ponder.

Worship or entertainment?

However, the main weakness of Evangelical Protestant worship isn't the musical forms it borrows from our culture, but the focus it encourages. The spotlight in much of Evangelical worship is not on God, but on the feelings aroused within the worshiper. The "praise the Lords" of its enthusiastic worship are often followed by a rhetorical question: "Don't it make you feel good?"[20] Having borrowed the musical styles of our culture, Evangelicalism has (perhaps inadvertently) borrowed its attitude as well. Worship has now become entertainment. The results in some corners of Evangelicalism have been extreme:

> [The Holy One of Israel has become] our buddy, our pal, our friend.... When a group of singers can gyrate all over the stage and croon sentimental mush about God the Father, God the Son, and God the Holy Spirit, and people clap and shout and stomp their feet, then surely our religion has been reduced to the lowest level of commercial entertainment.[21]

In spirit and truth

Worship forms are never ends in themselves. The Lutheran church never has insisted on uniform worship rites in all its congregations.[22] Nor is there any

176

virtue in worship conducted in a cold, detached, formalistic way as though there were something distasteful about human emotion. There's no correlation between a service's sterility and its orthodoxy. Confessional Lutherans aim to worship God in spirit as well as in truth (John 4:24).

Selling or proclaiming?

There's more at stake here than meets the eye. Worship is never merely a matter of personal taste. It's a travesty to see churches acting like fast food chains, each trying to get more customers by outdoing the others through advertising and packaging techniques. The gospel is not a product to be sold; it is a message to be proclaimed. It's time to ask whether the church in America today can afford to go on compromising the gospel by its consumer approach to worship. Has the gospel become just another sales pitch? Have we lowered God to the level of a media manipulator? Has he become just another used car salesman or fast-talking appliance store hawker in the public eye? This calls for sober evaluation and honest repentance.

There is another way of worship. It's the kind of worship which flows out of the gospel itself. Conservative Christians are concerned about orthodox preaching; it's time we take an active interest in orthodox worship as well. Here we can learn from other generations. In a similar age of decline in the church's worship life Wilhelm Loehe (d. 1872) stressed the intimate connection between doctrine and worship forms: "The true faith is expressed not only in the sermon but is also prayed in the prayers and sung in the hymns."[23]

Which response is, in fact, the most faithful to the gospel of Christ — the subjective, entertainment atmosphere encouraged in much of what passes for Christian worship today or objective praise of the God who comes to us in his Word and sacrament?

Mystery and understanding

I have demonstrated that God works in this world of ours in surprising ways: first in the incarnation of his Son, then in the word of the gospel, which from first to last is the message of Jesus Christ and him crucified. This word in both oral and sacramental form might be a stumbling block and foolishness to the unbeliever, but it is the very power and wisdom of God to those who are being saved (1 Corinthians 1:18-24).

The wisdom of God is hidden — hidden under the cross. There in lowly weakness God hid himself from human wisdom so that he might be more clearly known by those who believe in him. This is what the New Testament refers to as "mystery": that God reveals himself powerfully when he comes to us in the weakness of the cross of Christ. This mystery can never be grasped by human intellect; it is only revealed to those who trust in him.

No one is surprised when foreign visitors don't understand American football. There is nothing particularly logical about its rules. It has its own peculiar atmosphere and its own "liturgical" forms: cheerleaders, bands, officials, etc. Anyone can eventually become a football fan, but we don't expect everyone immediately to appreciate fully the game.

That's the way it works in football. For some strange reason, however, many have the idea that

Christian worship should be immediately accessible to the man off the street. If we take the New Testament seriously, we see this is impossible:

> The man without the Spirit does not accept the things that come from the Spirit of God, for they are foolishness to him, and he cannot understand them, because they are spiritually discerned. (1 Corinthians 2:14)

No wonder, then, that St. Paul wrote that those who hold the apostolic ministry should be regarded "as servants of Christ and stewards of the mysteries of God" (1 Corinthians 4:1[RSV]). The whole life of the church is caught up in the supernatural life God gives to his people through lowly natural channels: the oral word, water, bread and wine. We come to worship, then, not as we would go to a concert or a rally, expecting to be entertained. We come expecting to meet God. His Word and his sacrament throb with life and vitality. It is the life and vitality of God himself.

Barefoot worship

If worshiping with ancient liturgical forms seems unnatural to us, it is only because we have failed to grasp that we are in "unnatural" surroundings. Here, in this place and at this time, in, with, and under lowly natural means God has chosen to reveal the reality of his presence. Liturgical worship is the historic way the church has chosen to acknowledge the profound mystery of God's presence in its midst. These forms of worship may indeed seem unnatural to some, but this is the way the church removes its shoes; the place on which it stands is holy ground (Exodus 3:5).

Liturgical worship feels unnatural to us because it does not always reflect our "natural" feelings. Rather, it teaches us what to feel when God meets us in his Word and sacrament. F. H. Brabant has pointed out how we can "feel at home" with this kind of worship:

> All this demand for a worship which shall be the "natural" expression of what we feel, just like the demand for a devotional life always in the sunshine, without method or effort, is at bottom a confusion between the natural and the easy. We do not go to church to say and do "just as we like." . . . We come, stained and weary from a life that is largely unnatural, longing for something to lift us up into an atmosphere of spiritual peace. We ought, indeed, to "feel at home" in church, but we come to it as wanderers returned, not like tired city men calling for our slippers and our comfortable chairs. This is why we need all the help we can get from without, the steadiness of discipline, the beauty of holiness, the unswerving faith of the church, upon which to lean our poor half-heartedness. That is why the liturgy not only expresses what we feel; it also teaches us what we ought to feel.[24]

It's time to recognize Christian worship for what it is: Christ at work through his Word and sacrament. Rather than focusing on the mind and heart of the worshiper, worship should point to the God who meets us there. Growth in understanding worship comes along with growth in understanding his Word.[25]

Vitality in worship

Liturgical worship needn't be dull. What virtue is there in rattling through worship forms as if we were reading the telephone book? These are not merely outward forms. They represent a rich legacy. An appreciation of this liturgical legacy brings with it fresh energy and renewed vitality in every age. In the historic words of its liturgy the church joins with Christians of all time in giving praise to the God who has created, redeemed and sanctified it. There is after all only one church — both militant and triumphant, living here and living in heaven.

The triumphant echo

Like passengers on a train in a dark tunnel, Christians rejoice to be part of a vast company who have passed through the darkness of this world into the brilliant sunshine of God's glory. This means that worship is always an echo of the distant triumph song of those who even now rest from their labors in God's eternal presence. Such worship can be many things, but never listless or lifeless.

Finally, a revitalization of incarnational and sacramental theology will lead to a revitalization of our worship. Contemporary Christians live in a complex world. We face loneliness and anxiety in a world that becomes increasingly hostile as the years go by. We need a way to come into real contact with God. Can entertainment-centered worship provide that contact?

Reality in worship

The Lutheran church has a rich legacy to offer in its worship. Here is reality, not symbolism. Here we have real contact with God; not as we come to him, but as he comes to us. He meets us in the proclamation of the Word. Here the Son of God distributes his actual body and blood for the assurance of the forgiveness of sins. Here the people of God gather to offer him their thanks, their praise and their prayer.[26] This is the real thing!

It's time for a new initiative in worship. People are longing for God. Where are they going to find him? In the shifting sands of their inner life or on the solid rock of the word of his gospel? How are they to offer him their thanks and praise? With trivial methods borrowed from the entertainment industry or in worship forms which focus on the praise of God's gracious glory? This is the kind of worship which lifts the heart while it exalts Christ! And this is what Lutheran worship does.

Life as worship

The Christian faith, however, is not only a matter of *cultus*, or formal worship. It is also a matter of culture. There are direct lines leading from the sanctuary to the work place. Too frequently Lutheran Christians have failed to make that connection.

Piety need not be Pietism. It's significant that Luther included a table of duties for Christians of various vocations in his catechism. The life which we live in Christ as he lives through us is to be lived in the context of society, not only in the church. It's significant, for example, that along with suggested prayers for morning and evening his catechism prescribes the signing of the cross. This was no mechanical formalism, nor some sort of superstitious magic. This action was a vivid reminder that each day is begun, continued and ended in the death and resurrection of our baptism. Our whole life is a life under the cross of Christ.

The gospel is not only a message; it brings with it a whole new way of looking at life and living it. It is life style Christianity, but it's a life style freed from the constraints of the legal demands and the plastic superficiality that characterize too much of American Christianity in our day. This life style is nothing less than Christ in action. It is Jesus Christ living out his life in his people!

CONCLUSION

This book began as an academic exercise; it turned out to be a personal pilgrimage. Other more theological minds will have to judge how well I have succeeded at articulating Lutheran teaching. I only hope that something here will offer renewed hope and promise to people looking for God in their world.

There are, after all, only two places to look for God: in your heart or in his gospel. I hope I have demonstrated that the heart is the wrong place to look.

For all of its zeal and enthusiasm for Jesus, most of American Evangelicalism ends up pointing people to their hearts to find God. Jesus may have saved us, but now it's basically up to us to live for him. *If* we commit our lives to him, *if* we surrender control to him, *if* we have victory over sin — only then we may be sure that we are his.

But there is another place to look for God. The gospel is actually the only place God has promised to be found. This gospel comes to us in many ways: in

183

preaching, sacraments and absolution. In each case, however, the gospel has one content, and one content only: Jesus Christ and him crucified. For God hides under the cross to reveal himself more clearly to us. In his death he demonstrates that sin is destroyed and the grave has no power over us. The cross of Christ gives life to the world.

And our life in Christ is a life under his cross. Day by day our sinful nature goes on dying and we go on living with him. This is why the Christian life is not really the Christian in action; it is Christ in action!

This, I can assure you, is not just theory. It is reality, the reality of God at work in this world of ours through his Word and sacraments. Continually that reality becomes more clear to me. This is my personal pilgrimage. And I hope it will be yours.

> Oh, it is a living, busy, active, mighty thing, this faith! It is impossible for it not to be doing good works incessantly. It does not ask whether good works are to be done, but before the question is asked, it has already done them, and is constantly doing them.

> Faith is a living, daring confidence in God's grace, so sure and certain that the believer would stake his life on it a thousand times. This knowledge of and confidence in God's grace makes men glad and bold and happy in dealing with God and with all creatures. And this is the work which the Holy Spirit performs in faith. Because of it, without compulsion, a person is ready and glad to do good to everyone, to suffer everything, out of love and praise to God who has shown him this grace.

> Martin Luther, *Preface to Romans*

NOTES

1. American Christianity in the Eighties: A Focus on Life Style

1. Kathy Sawyer, "New Christians: Is Fundamentalism a Search for Truth or Moral McCarthyism?" Madison WI *Capital Times*, 2 January 1985, p. 1.

2. Virginia Stem Owens, *The Total Image*, (Grand Rapids: Eerdmans, 1980), p. 27

3. Carol Flake, *Redemptorama: Culture, Politics and the New Evangelicalism*, Garden City NY: Anchor Press, 1984). p. 22.

4. The term "Evangelical" or "Evangelicalism" in the rest of this study will be used without quotation marks as references to the current heirs of Fundamentalism in America. As mentioned above, the adjective evangelical has a separate history and meaning within both Lutheran and Reformed orthodoxy.

5. Martin H. Scharlemann, "Fundamentalism," *Affirm*, 9:5 (February-March, 1982), p. 2.

6. Richard John Neuhaus, "What the Fundamentalists Want," *Commentary*, May, 1985, p. 42.

7. Irving Louis Horowitz, "Revolt Against Modernity: The New Fundamentalism," *Society* (November/December 1982):46.

8. Jeremy Rifkin with Ted Howard, *The Emerging Order: God in the Age of Scarcity* (New York: G. P. Putnam's Sons, 1979), p. 202.

9. Richard Quebedeaux, *The New Charismatics II*, (San Francisco: Harper & Row, 1983), p. xv.

10. Walther von Loewenich, *Luther's Theology of the Cross*, trans. Herbert J. A. Bouman (Minneapolis: Augsburg, 1976), p. 124.

11. All quotations from the Lutheran Confessions are from *The Book of Concord* trans. and ed. Th. G. Tappert (St. Louis: Concordia, 1959).

12. See chapters 5 and 6.

13. John 1:1,14; Hebrews 1:1,2.

14. Matthew 18:20; John 6:63; 1 John 5:11.

15. Luther: "This monster of uncertainty surpasses all other monsters. . . . Let us therefore give thanks to God that we are delivered from this monstrous doctrine of doubting. This is our foundation: The gospel commands us to behold not our own good works, our own perfection, but God, the Promiser, and Christ, the Mediator, etc." Quoted in Francis Pieper, *Christian Dogmatics*, 3 vols. (St. Louis: Concordia, 1951), 2:550.

16. Bruce L. Shelley, *Evangelicalism in America* (Grand Rapids: Eerdmans, 1967).

17. Flake, *Redemptorama*, p. 61.

18. This term will be addressed in chapter 6.

19. Owens. *The Total Image*, p. 76.

20. Gregory Lewis, *Is God for Sale?: A Provocative Examination of Today's Church* (Wheaton IL: Tyndale, 1979), p. 127.

21. Bethlehem Lutheran Church, Sun Prairie WI, presentation by former members of the Lutheran Church — Missouri Synod, April, 1986.

22. C. F. W. Walther, *Convention Essays* (St. Louis: Concordia, 1981) p. 19, quoted in David Valleskey, "Evangelical Lutheranism and Today's Evangelicals and Fundamentalists," *Wisconsin Lutheran Quarterly*, 80:219.

23. 1) The Word of God, 2) Sin, death, hell and damnation, 3) Divine providence, 4) Universal grace, 5) Reconciliation and redemption of the human race, 6) Justification by faith, 7) Regeneration and sanctification, 8) Means of grace, 9) Conversion, 10) Prayer, 11) Obedience toward men in matters of faith and conscience, 12) Election. Listed in Vallesky, loc. cit.

2. The Roots of Evangelicalism

1. Named after its founder, Jacobus Arminius (d. 1609), Arminianism is characterized by its emphasis on free will over against divine election as the cause of salvation. Calvinists, on the other hand, believed that God had chosen (elected) some to be saved and some to be damned. According to this view, Jesus died to save only the elect.

2. For a discussion of contemporary movements characterized as the "religious right," see Samuel S. Hill & Dennis E. Owen, *The New Religious Right in America* (Nashville: Abingdon, 1982).

3. John Winthrop's sermon aboard the *Mayflower*, quoted in Rifkin, *The Emerging Order*, p. 131.

4. John Calvin taught that God had predestined some of mankind to salvation and others to damnation — both to the praise of his glory and in accordance with his sovereign will.

5. An earlier example of this kind of strict Calvinism is found in this excerpt of a 1726 sermon by Jonathan Edwards: "We must come off from this (pride) to an absolute despair of helping ourselves, either in purchasing redemption for ourselves, or in applying the redemption already purchased. We must leave all hoping that we shall be able either to satisfy God's justice or to bring ourselves to a hearty acceptance of Christ's satisfaction. We must not imagine that we of our own ability shall either convert ourselves or uphold ourselves in a state of grace or do any good work of ourselves when we are converted." Unpublished manuscript in the library of Yale University quoted in Wells and Woodbridge, *The Evangelicals — What They Believe, Who They Are, Where They are Changing* (Nashville: Abingdon, 1975), p. 36.

6. James Hastings Nichols, *History of Christianity 1650-1950*, (New York: The Ronald Press, 1956), p. 191.

7. Kenneth Scott Latourette, *A History of Christianity* (New York: Harper & Row, 1953), p. 1037.

8. Bruce L. Shelley, *Evangelicalism in America*, p. 47.

9. George M. Marsden, *Fundamentalism and American Culture* (New York: Oxford University Press, 1980), p. 99f.

10. Nichols, *History of Christianity*, p. 195.

11. W. A. Stearns, President of Amherst College, in a speech to the Evangelical Alliance of 1873 quoted in Marsden, *Fundamentalism and American Culture*, p. 17.

12. Shelley, *Evangelicalism in America*, p. 46.

13. From a sermon of D. L. Moody quoted in Rifkin, *The Emerging Order*, p. 155.

14. From Spener's *Dreyzehn Theologische Sendschreiben*, 1716, quoted in Lindberg, *The Third Reformation*, p. 145.

15. For a discussion of this theme, see Walter von Loewenich, *Luther's Theology of the Cross* (Minneapolis: Augsburg, 1976).

16. John Wesley's account of his "Aldersgate experience," quoted in Shelley, *Evangelicalism in America*, p. 36.

17. Methodism was so named because of its emphasis on "methods," or disciplinary guidelines, for the new life.

18. For a discussion of this theme, see Bengt Hägglund, *History of Theology*, trans. Gene J. Lund (St. Louis: Concordia, 1968), pp. 325-334.

19. Luther, *Against the Heavenly Prophets*, LW 40, p. 146.

20. Shelley, *Evangelicalism in America*, p. 49.

21. "While Luther placed sanctification under the umbrella of justification, Wesley set sanctification alongside justification. In later revivalism justification was virtually absorbed into sanctification." Donald G. Bloesch, *Essentials of Evangelical Theology* Vol. II (San Francisco: Harper & Row, 1978), p. 45.

22. Marsden, *Fundamentalism and American Culture*, p. 78.

23. Nichols, *History of Christianity*, p. 273.

24. Wells and Woodbridge, *The Evangelicals*, p. 12.

25. Shelley, *Evangelicalism in America*, p. 120.

26. See below, "The Evangelical Initiative: Cultural Sensitivity," p. 49.

27. *The Late Great Planet Earth* and *Satan is Alive and Well on Planet Earth*.

28. Marsden, *Evangelicalism and Modern America*, p. ix f.

29. *Excursus:* Many Evangelicals themselves appear to classify conservative Lutherans within their ranks:

> . . . evangelical broadcasts such as The Lutheran Hour, the Hour of Decision, Back to the Bible Hour, and The Old Fashioned Revival Hour continue to proclaim the Word of Truth. (Shelley, *Evangelicalism in America*, p. 92)

George Marsden, though he acknowledges that "Among Lutherans, 'evangelical' has a more general meaning (than elsewhere in American Protestantism) . . . " (Marsden, *Evangelicalism and Modern America*, p. x) still asserts that certain Lutherans in America can be considered part of the Fundamentalist phenomena:

> Other denominations, including the Lutheran Church — Missouri Synod and the Christian Reformed, were also Americanized to an extent by adopting some Fundamentalist ideals while retaining other distinctive features of their European traditions.

Milton Rudnick, having set out for proof of the Lutheran Church — Missouri Synod complicity with Fundamentalism, was unable to prove his thesis after consulting the evidence: "The conclusion is that Fundamentalism and the Missouri Synod were not related closely enough for either one to exert major and lasting influence on the other." (Rudnick, *Fundamentalism and the Missouri Synod*, [St. Louis: Concordia, 1966], p. 115)

Donald Bloesch handles the tension between the fact of common doctrinal conclusions and their differing roots among conservative Lutherans and American Evangelicals by listing the former as "confessionalist evangelicals." Consequently, he categorizes the two seminaries of the LCMS together with Calvin Theological Seminary, Wisconsin Lutheran Seminary and Reformed Theological Seminary as "evangelical within a confessionalist context" (Bloesch, *The Future of Evangelical Christianity*, p. 36). In addition, he lumps together a group who might likely consider themselves strange bedfellows:

> Theologians in recent times who would identify themselves as confessionalist evangelicals include Fred Klooster, Horace Hummel, Anthony Hoekema, Cornelius Van Til, Martin Scharlemann, Edmund Schlink, Robert Preus, David

Scaer, Paul Althaus, Ford Lewis Battles, G. C. Berkouwer, Peter Beyerhaus, Gerhard Maier and Walter Kunneth. (Ibid.)

To be fair, when ranged in opposition to a liberal Christendom which is all too often a thinly veiled agnosticism, conservative Lutherans could indeed be considered "Evangelical" in the American Protestant sense. David Scaer has pointed out the unacknowledged debt owed by Missouri Synod Lutherans to Evangelical scholars in facing up to its crisis in Biblical theology ("Lutheran Viewpoints on the Challenge of Fundamentalism: Eschatology," *Concordia Journal*, January 1984, pp 4-6).

Perhaps the best way to describe the relationship between these distinct, but in many ways sympathetic, theological systems is to resurrect a two-word adjectival phrase which historically described the Lutheran church: "Evangelical Lutheran."

30. " ... neither renewal, sanctification, virtues, nor other good works are our righteousness before God, nor are they to be made and posited to be a part or a cause of our justification, nor under any kind of pretense, title, or name are they to be mingled with the article of justification as pertinent or necessary to it. The righteousness of faith consists solely in the forgiveness of sins by sheer grace, entirely for the sake of Christ's merit, which treasures are offered to us in the promise of the gospel and received, accepted, applied to us, and made our own solely through faith" (Formula of Concord, Solid Declaration III [39]).

31. Quoted by Francis Schaeffer, "Truth Versus the New Humanism and the New Theology" in *Evangelical Directions for the Lutheran Church*, Erich Kiehl and Waldo J. Werning, eds., n.p., n.d., p. 28.

32. Marsden. *Fundamentalism and American Culture*, p. 20.

33. Rifkin, *The Emerging Order*, p. 7.

34. *Ibid.*, p. 137.

35. *Ibid.*, p. 129.

36. Bloesch. *The Future of Evangelical Christianity*, p. 2.

37. Neuhaus. "What the Fundamentalists Want," *Commentary* (May, 1985), p. 42.

38. Shelley, *Evangelicalism in America*, p. 113.

39. "These scholars (Carl Henry, et al.) of the Evangelical movement provided much of the exegetical and theological building materials for those in the Missouri Synod who were concerned with re-establishing the Synod's traditional stance." David P. Scaer, "Lutheran Viewpoints on the Challenge of Fundamentalism," p. 6.

40. Bloesch, *Essentials of Evangelical Theology*, Vol. II, p. 267.

41. Bloesch, *The Future of Evangelical Christianity*, p. 7.

42. Bloesch, *The Evangelical Renaissance*, p. 18.

43. Rifkin, *The Emerging Order*, p. 228.

44. See above, p. 40.

45. Owens, *The Total Image*, pp. 4f.

46. Flake, *Redemptorama*, pp. 175f.

47. Rifkin, *The Emerging Order*, p. 105.

48. Owens, *The Total Image*, p. 28.

49. *Ibid.*, pp. 36f.

50. Bloesch, *The Future of Evangelical Christianity*, p. 103.

51. Rifkin, *The Emerging Order*, p. 125.

52. For a discussion of this subject, see Leonard I. Sweet, "The 1960s: The Crises of Liberal Christianity and the Public Emergence of Evangelicalism," George Marsden, ed. *Evangelicalism and Modern America*, pp. 29-45.

53. Bloesch, *The Evangelical Renaissance*, p. 37.

3. The Christian in Action: Sanctification in Selected Writings of Charles Swindoll

1. Lutherans, on the other hand, have written many more scholarly than popular works. The New Evangelicals seem to have learned more from Luther than his namesakes; his popular pamphlets and hymns had a greater demonstrable effect in spreading the Evangelical message than his professional theological efforts.

2. Information from Word Publishing, Inc., December 1988.

3. It is not surprising that Swindoll should mention the glory of God among the purposes of the renewed life. This is a prominent theme in the thought of John Calvin, the great Swiss theologian whose work is the foundation of Reformed theology. Contemporary Evangelicalism is deeply indebted to its Reformed ancestry.

4. Each of the three books under study will be indicated with initials followed by the page reference:

I.S. = Charles Swindoll, *Improving Your Serve* (Waco TX: Word, 1981).
S.G. = Charles Swindoll, *Strengthening Your Grip* (Waco TX: Word, 1982).
D.G. = Charles Swindoll, *Dropping Your Guard* (Waco TX: Word, 1983).

5. Quotation from Frank B. Minirth and Paul Meier, *Happiness is a Choice* (Grand Rapids: Baker, 1978).

6. Quoting J. Oswald Sanders, *Spiritual Leadership* (Chicago: Moody Press, 1967), p. 142.

4. Life Style Christianity Examined

1. In this chapter, as in the previous one, references from Swindoll's books will be indicated by initials followed by page reference:

I.S. = Charles Swindoll, *Improving Your Serve* (Waco TX: Word, 1981).
S.G. = Charles Swindoll, *Strengthening Your Grip* (Waco TX: Word, 1982).
D.G. = Charles Swindoll, *Dropping Your Guard* (Waco TX: Word, 1983).

2. Bruce Larson and Keith Miller, *The Edge of Adventure* (Waco TX: Word, 1974), p. 156, quoted in D.G., 128).

3. This is a distinctly Calvinist theme. Eckhardt comments: "[John Calvin] calls justification the 'main hinge,' he calls its two benefits reconciliation to God and being 'sanctified by

Christ's spirit [that] we may cultivate blamelessness and purity of life.' Since the acknowledgement of God's sovereignty is seen as having highest importance, justification must be understood as a preliminary step to this end. Therefore obedience has more value to God than faith, though it is necessary for faith to be present before obedience can begin." (Burnell F. Eckardt Jr., "The Wrath of God in the Theology of John Calvin" (M.S.T. thesis, Concordia Theological Seminary, Ft. Wayne IN, 1983), p. 45.

4. See chapter 6.

5. The Lutheran Confessions teach that God is actually working in and through baptism: "the grace of God is offered through Baptism" (A.C. IX, 2). Baptism is "efficacious for salvation." (Apol. IX, 1).

6. See chapter 5, the section "Life Under the Cross."

7. Advertising insert for *Living on the Ragged Edge*, in *Guideposts*, February, 1986.

8. See chapter 3.

5. Christ in Action: A Lutheran View of Sanctification, More Than a Life Style

1. Adolf Koeberle, *The Quest for Holiness* (Minneapolis: Augsburg, 1938; reprint ed., St. Louis: Concordia Heritage Series, 1982), p. 259.

2. Bloesch, *Essentials of Evangelical Theology*, Vol. II, p. 276.

3. Lindberg, *The Third Reformation* pp. 140f.

4. *Luther's Works* [hereafter LW], Vol. 34, 336f.

5. Luther, *Small Catechism*, 1986 translation, St. Louis: Concordia, 1986, pp. 16,17.

6. Luther, Sermon on 1 Corinthians 15:1ff, March 31, 1529, quoted in Adolf Koeberle, *The Quest for Holiness*, p. 79.

7. See chapter 1, the section "The Evangelical attraction: personal experience as proof of faith."

8. Lindberg, *The Third Reformation?*, p. 180.

9. Scaer "Sanctification in Lutheran Theology," *Concordia Theological Quarterly*, 49:2,3, p. 188.

10. David Scaer explains: " ... the life of the Christian is the life of Christ in the world, that is, it tells us what Christ is doing now." op. cit., p. 194.

11. Luther, LW 34, p. 111.

12. Luther, *Lectures on Galatians*, LW 26, 29.

13. I am indebted to Robert Kolb for his summary of this and many other aspects of Luther's "Theology of the Cross."

14. Luther: "On the other hand we must understand the nature of Christ's office and work in his church, that while he pours out his purity on us at once, through the Word and faith, and, in addition, renews our hearts through the Holy Ghost, he does this in such a way that this work of purification is not completed all at once, but he daily labors with us and purifies us so that we become continuously purer and purer." Quoted in Adolf Koeberle, *The Quest for Holiness*, p. 152.

15. C. S. Lewis, *Mere Christianity* (New York: MacMillian, 1960), p. 174.

16. Luther, "Explanations of the Ninety-five Theses", LW 31, p. 225,226.

6. Christ in Action: The Sacraments, Absolution and Worship

1. Robert E. Webber, *Evangelicals on the Canterbury Trail*: Why Evangelicals are Attracted to the Liturgical Church (Waco TX: Jarrell, 1985), p. 51.

2. Owens, *The Total Image*, p. 55.

3. 1 Corinthians 2:7.

4. Luther, *Against the Heavenly Prophets*, LW 40, p. 146.

5. Luther explains in his *Small Catechism* the necessity of faith in the sacraments (in baptism): "Water certainly does not do them [provide the spiritual benefits], but the word of God in and with the water; and faith, which trusts this word of God in the water." (In Communion): "It is not eating and drinking that does them, of course, but the words: 'Given and shed for you for the forgiveness of sins.' Along with the bodily eating and drink-

ing, these words are the main thing in the sacrament. Whoever believes these words has exactly what they say: 'forgiveness of sins.' "

6. Koeberle, *The Quest for Holiness*, p. 63.

7. *The Small Catechism*, 1986 translation, St. Louis: Concordia, 1986, pp. 16,17.

8. Bruce L. Blackie, *Gods of Goodness The Sophisticated Idolatry of the Main Line Churches* (Philadelphia: Westminster, 1975), pp. 88f.

9. Koeberle, *The Quest for Holiness*, pp. 67f.

10. Early Lutherans understood the sacrament to be a focal point of both corporate worship and personal spirituality: "We are unjustly accused of having abolished the Mass. Without boasting, it is manifest that the Mass is observed among us with greater devotion and more earnestness than among our opponents" (AC XXIV. The Mass, Tappert, p. 56).

11. David F. Wells and John D. Woodbridge, eds., *The Evangelicals — What They Believe, Who They Are, Where They are Changing* (Nashville: Abingdon, 1975), p. 35.

12. Althaus sums up Luther's view: " ... good works can be done only by the man who already has a good conscience because God has freely forgiven his sin. A good conscience is not the product but the source of the Christian ethos." Paul Althaus, Robert C. Schultz, trans. *The Ethics of Martin Luther* (Philadelphia: Fortress, 1972), p. 4.

13. Early Lutheran practice may be our guide: " ... people are carefully instructed concerning the consolation of the word of absolution so that they may esteem absolution as a great and precious thing. It is not the voice or word of the man who speaks it, but it is the word of God, who forgives sin, for it's spoken in God's stead and by God's command. We teach with great diligence about this command and power of keys and how comforting and necessary it is for terrified consciences. We also teach that God requires us to believe this absolution as much as if we heard God's voice from heaven, that we should joyfully comfort ourselves with absolution, and that we should know that through such faith we obtain forgiveness of sins" (*Augsburg Confession*, Article XXV. "Confession" par. 2-4).

14. Luther, "Confession," *Large Catechism*, par. 32,33.

15. Dietrich Bonhoeffer, Jay C. Rochelle, trans. *Spiritual Care* (Philadelphia: Fortress Press, 1982), p. 63.

16. Luther, LW 36, p. 86.

17. IV. "The Gospel", *Smalcald Articles*, p. 310.

18. Dietrich Bonhoeffer, John Doberstein, trans., *Life Together* (San Francisco: Harper & Row, 1954), p. 110.

19. Wilhelm Loehe, "Einfaeltiger Beichtunterricht," *Gesammelte Werke*, Neuendettelsau: Freimund Verlag, 1951, p. 165.

20. For a discussion of Evangelical worship see Virginia Owen, *The Total Image*, p. 63ff.

21. Webber, *Common Roots*, p. 221.

22. "It is not necessary for the true unity of the Christian church that ceremonies, instituted by men, should be observed uniformly in all places." (Augsburg Confession, Article VII. "The Church", p. 3)

23. Willhelm Loehe, James Schaaf, trans., *Three Books About the Church* (Philadelphia: Fortress, 1969), p. 179.

24. F. H. Brabant, "Worship in General," *Liturgy and Worship* (London: S.P.C.K., 1933), p. 13.

25. The center of Christian worship is the mystery of the gospel. And the mystery of the gospel is grasped only by those to whom God has revealed himself in the cross of his Son, Jesus Christ. John Pless shows how the gospel is compromised when the liturgy is made intelligible to unbelievers.

> As the divine service has to do with the "mysteries of God" (1 Corinthians 4:1), it will not be readily understandable to the unbeliever. Indeed, the unbeliever cannot understand it. The solution is not to do away with the "mysteries of God" by transforming the divine service into a recruitment rally. Rather, the unbeliever is to be brought into the congregation through the washing of regeneration. In Matthew 28:19,20 teaching is connected with baptism. Disciples are made by baptism and teaching. . . . the liturgy is to be taught not simply as a collection of inherited forms, but as the rhythm of God's speaking and doing and our listening and receiving.

(John Pless, "Six Theses on Liturgy and Evangelism," *Concordia Theological Quarterly*, January, 1988, 51:1, p. 44)

26. Christian worship is for Christians. Contemporary worship is often used as a method of evangelism; the problem is that something has to give in such a situation; most often it is worship.

> . . . the historic Christian approach to worship which emphasizes the adoration of the Father through the Son has been replaced in some churches by a program with a stage and an audience. And the nature of worship as an offering up of the whole person, the entire community, the body, through the head, Jesus Christ, as a ministry of praise to the Father has been replaced by an emphasis which sees the minister as the agent of God to evangelize the lost and teach the saints.
>
> (Webber, op. cit., p. 78).

Guests at worship can be made to feel welcome by the worshipers before and after the service. Friendliness and winsomeness are not incompatible with liturgical worship!

SELECTED BIBLIOGRAPHY

Books

Althaus, Paul. *The Ethics of Martin Luther*. Trans. Robert Schultz. Philadelphia: Fortress Press, 1972.

Barr, James. *Fundamentalism*. London: SCM Press, 1977.

Bloesch, Donald G. *The Evangelical Renaissance*. Grand Rapids: Eerdmans, 1973.

———. *Essentials of Evangelical Theology*. Vol. One: God, Authority, and Salvation, San Francisco: Harper & Row, 1978.

———. *Essentials of Evangelical Theology*. Vol. Two: Life, Ministry, and Hope, San Francisco: Harper & Row, 1979.

———. *The Future of Evangelical Christianity: A Call for Unity amid Diversity*. Garden Grove NY: Doubleday, 1983.

Bonhoeffer, Dietrich *Life Together* Trans. John Doberstein, San Francisco: Harper & Row, 1954.

———. *Spiritual Care* Trans. Jay C. Rochelle, Philadelphia: Fortress Press, 1982.

Brabant, Frank Herbert, "Worship in General", Clarke, W. K., and Harris, Charles, eds. *Liturgy and Worship* A Companion to the Prayer Books of the Anglican Communion London: Society for Promoting Christian Knowledge, 1933.

Branson, Mark Lau, *The Reader's Guide to the Best Evangelical Books*. San Francisco: Harper & Row, 1982.

Cooper, John Charles. *The Turn Right*. Philadelphia: Westminster, 1970.

Clabaugh, Gary K. *Thunder on the Right: the Protestant Fundamentalists*. Chicago: Nelson-Hall Co., 1974.

Clouse, Robert G. *The Cross & the Flag*. Carol Stream IL: Creation House, 1972.

Dayton, Donald W. *Discovering an Evangelical Heritage*. New York: Harper & Row, 1976.

Douglas, James Dixon, ed. *Evangelicals and Unity*. Appleford, England: Marcham Manor Press, 1964.

Eckardt, Burnell F., Jr. "The Wrath of God in the Theology of John Calvin." S.T.M. Thesis, Concordia Theological Seminary, Ft. Wayne IN, 1983.

Fackre, Gabriel. *The Religious Right and christian Faith*. Grand Rapids: Eerdmans, 1982.

Flake, Carol, *Redemptorama: Culture, Politics and the New Evangelicalism*. Garden City NY: Anchor Press, 1984.

Feinberg, Charles L., ed. *The Fundamentals for Today*. Grand Rapids: Kegel, 1961.

Fuller, David Otis, ed. *Valiant for the Truth: A Treasury of Evangelical Writings*. New York: McGraw-Hill, 1961.

Gasper, Louis. *The Fundamentalist Movement*. The Hague: Mouton, 1963.

Gilquist, Peter E. *The Physical Side of Being Spiritual*. Grand Rapids: Zondervan, 1979.

Hägglund, Bengt. *History of Theology*. Trans. Gene Lund St. Louis: Concordia, 1968.

Henry, Carl F. *Evangelical Responsibility in Contemporary Theology*. Grand Rapids: Eerdmans, 1957.

_____ . *Evangelicals at the Brink of Crisis: Significance of the World Congress on Evangelism*. Waco TX: Word, 1967.

_____ . ed. *Christian Faith and Modern Theology: Contemporary Evangelical Thought*. New York: Channel Press, 1957.

_____ . ed. *Fundamentals of the Faith*. Grand Rapids: Zondervan, 1969.

_____ . ed. *Revelation and the Bible: Contemporary Evangelical Thought*. Grand Rapids: Baker, 1958.

Hill, Samuel S. & Owen, Dennis E. *The New Religious Political Right in America*. Nashville: Abingdon, 1982.

Inch, Morris A. *The Evangelical Challenge.* Philadelphia: Westminster, 1978.

Johnston, Robert K. *Evangelicals at an Impasse: Biblical Authority in Practice.* Atlanta: John Knox, 1979.

Jorstad, Erling T. *The Politics of Doomsday: Fundamentalists of the Far Right.* Nashville: Abingdon, 1970.

Koeberle, Adolf. *The Quest for Holiness.* Trans. John C. Mattes. Minneapolis: Augsburg, 1936, Concordia Heritage Series, 1982.

Lindberg, Carter. *The Third Reformation?* Charismatic Movements and the Lutheran Tradition. Macon, Georgia: Mercer University Press, 1983.

Loehe, Wilhelm. *Gesammelte Werke.* Neuendettelsau: Freimund-Verlag, 1951.

_____. *Three Books About the Church.* Trans. James L. Schaaf. Philadelphia: Fortress, 1969.

von Loewenich, Walther. *Luther's Theology of the Cross.* Herbert J. A. Bouman, trans. Minneapolis: Augsburg, 1976.

Lovelace, Richard F. *Dynamics of Spiritual Life: An Evangelical Theology of Renewal.* Downers Grove IL: Inter-varsity Press, 1979.

Macintosh, Douglas Clyde. *Personal Religion.* New York: Scribner, 1942.

Marsden, George. *Fundamentalism and American Culture: The Shaping of Twentieth Century Evangelicalism 1870 —1925.* New York: Oxford University Press, 1980.

_____. ed. *Evangelicalism and Modern America.* Grand Rapids: Eerdmans, 1984.

Marty, Martin E. *The Public Church: Mainline, Evangelical, Catholic.* New York: Crossroad, 1981.

Nash, Ronald H. *The New Evangelicalism.* Grand Rapids: Zondervan, 1963.

Owens, Virginia Stem. *The Total Image: Selling Jesus in the Modern Age.* Grand Rapids: Eerdmans, 1980.

Pieper, Francis. *Christian Dogmatics.* 4 vols. St. Louis: Concordia, 1953. Vol. 3.

Proctor, Wm. *The Born-Again Christian Catalog: a Complete Sourcebook for Evangelicals*. New York: M. Evans, 1979.

Quebedeaux, Richard. *The Worldy Evangelicals*. San Francisco: Harper & Row, 1976.

_____ . *The Young Evangelicals: Revolution in Orthodoxy*. New York: Harper & Row, 1974.

_____ . *The New Charismatics II*. New York: Harper & Row, 1983.

Ramm, Bernard. *The Evangelical Heritage*. Waco TX: Word, 1973.

Rogers, Jack Bartlett. *Confessions of a Conservative Evangelical*. Philadelphia: Westminster, 1974.

Russell, Charles Allen. *Voice of American Fundamentalism: Seven Biographical Studies*. Philadelphia: Westminster, 1976.

Sandeen, Ernest R. *The Roots of Fundamentalism: British and American Millenarianism 1800-1930*. Chicago: University of Chicago Press, 1970.

Sasse, Hermann. *We Confess*. Vol. 1: Jesus Christ. Trans. Norman Nagel. St. Louis: Concordia, 1984.

_____ . *We Confess*. Vol. 2: The Sacraments. Trans. Norman Nagel. St. Louis: Concordia, 1985.

_____ . *We Confess*. Vol. 3: The Church. Trans. Norman Nagel St. Louis: Concordia, 1986.

Schlink, Edmund. *Theology of the Lutheran Confessions*. Trans. Paul Koehneke and Herbert Bouman. Philadelphia: Fortress, 1961.

Shelley, Bruce Leon. *Evangelicalism in America*. Grand Rapids: Eerdmans, 1967.

Staehlin, Wilhelm. *The Mystery of God. The Presence of God with Men*. St. Louis: Concordia Publishing House, 1964.

Stevick, Daniel B. *Beyond Fundamentalism*. Richmond: John Knox Press, 1964.

Stott, John R. W. *Fundamentalism and Evangelism*. Grand Rapids: Eerdmans, 1959.

Swindoll, Charles R. *Improving Your Serve: The Art of Unselfish Living*. Waco TX: Word, 1981.

_____ . *Strengthening Your Grip: Essentials in an Aimless World*. Waco TX: Word, 1982.

_____ . *Dropping Your Guard: The Value of Open Relationships*. Waco TX: Word, 1983.

Tenny, Merrill C., ed *The Word for This Century*. New York: Oxford Univ. Press, 1960.

Watson, Philip S., *Let God be God!*. Philadelphia: Muhlenberg Press, 1949.

Webber, Robert. *Common Roots: A Call to Evangelical Maturity*. Grand Rapids: Zondervan, 1978.

_____ . *Evangelicals on the Canterbury Trail*. Why Evangelicals are Attracted to the Liturgical Church. Waco TX: Word, 1985.

Wells, Wm. W. *Welcome to the Family: An Introduction to Evangelical Christianity*. Downers Grove IL: Inter-varsity Press, 1979.

Wells, Wm., and Woodbridge, John, ed. *The Evangelicals: What They Believe, Who They Are, Where They Are Changing*. Nashville: Abingdon, 1975.

Witte, Paul W. *On Common Ground: Protestant and Catholic Evangelicals*. Waco TX: Word, 1975.

Woodbridge, John D. *The Gospel in America: Themes in the Story of America's Evangelicals*. Grand Rapids: Zondervan. 1979.

Articles

Gordis, R. "The Revival of Religion and the Decay of Ethics." *Christianity Today*, 28 (June 15, 1984), 30.

Horowitz, I. L. "The New Fundamentalism." *Society*, 20 (1982) 40-47.

Ji, Won Yong. "Issues Facing Today's Ministry." *Concordia Journal*, 12:2 (March 1986), 41-42.

_____ . "The Work of the Holy Spirit and the Charismatic Movements, from Luther's Perspective." *Concordia Journal* 11:6 (November, 1985), 214-222.

Kantzer, K. S. "Evangelicalism: Midcourse Appraisal." *Christianity Today*, 27 (June 7, 1983), 10-11.

Kraft, Charles H. "Can Anthropological Insight Assist Evangelical Theology?" *Christian Scholar's Review* (165-202).

Lovelace, R. L. "Completing an Awakening." *Christian Century*, 98 (March 18, 1981), 296-300.

McDonnell, Kilian. "A Catholic Looks at Evangelical Protestantism." *Commonweal* 92 (1970), 408-413.

Marty, Martin E. "Addition to the Dictionary." *Christian Century*, 102 (July 31-August 7, 1985) 719.

Mylott, Kenneth J. "Unplugging the Electronic 'Church'." *Lutheran Forum*, 20:1 (Lent 1986) 14-15.

Montgomery, J. W. "Born-Againism: An Evangelical Innovation?" *Christianity Today*, 26 (October 22, 1982), 80.

Neuhaus, Richard J. "What the Fundamentalists Want." *Commentary* 80 (May, 1985), 12-15.

_____ . "The Conservative Tradition and the Prophetic Ideal." *Agenda for a Prophetic Faith* Annual Lecture Series. Madison, Wisconsin, 12 February 1986.

Ostling, Richard N. "Power, Glory — And Politics (Right-wing preachers dominate the dial)." *Time*, 17 February 1986, 62-69.

Pless, John T. "Six Theses on Liturgy and Evangelism." *Concordia Theological Quarterly* 52:1 (January 1988), 41-52.

Scaer, David P. "Lutheran Viewpoints on the Challenge of Fundamentalism: Eschatology." *Concordia Journal* (1984), 4-11.

_____ . "Sanctification in Lutheran Theology." *Concordia Theological Quarterly* 49 (1985): 181-197.

Shelley, B. L., "Will American Evangelicalism Survive?" *Christianity Today* 28 (June 15, 1984) 30.

Valleskey, David. "Evangelical Lutheranism and Today's Evangelicals and Fundamentalists" *Wisconsin Lutheran Quarterly*, Vol. 80, Number 3 (Summer, 1983): 180-220.

Wente, Dean O. "The Flesh & Blood Spirit." *Lutheran Witness*, Vol. 105, Number 3 (March, 1986): 1, 14-15.

"The Born-Again Movement: A Response," Division of Theological Studies, Lutheran Council in the USA, March 1984, 12pp.